FLOYD SHAFFER is well-known to church groups and other audiences across the country through his pioneering work in clown ministry. The pastor of a Detroit congregation, he has performed his ministry as Socataco the Clown before more than 40 different Christian denominations. He has been featured in *Time, Newsweek,* and on "P.M. Magazine," and has appeared in three religious films.

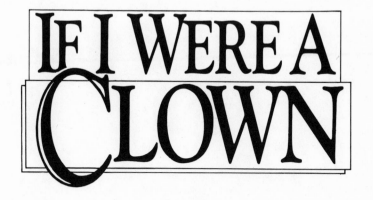

IF I WERE A CLOWN

FLOYD SHAFFER

AUGSBURG Publishing House • Minneapolis

IF I WERE A CLOWN

Scripture quotations unless otherwise noted are from the Holy Bible: New International Version. Copyright 1978 by the New York International Bible Society. Used by permission of Zondervan Bible Publishers.

Photos: William Mitchell, 1, 14, 22, 31, 38, 44, 58, 65, 67, 82, 86, 92; James J. Baron, 27, 76; Hildegard Adler, 72.

Library of Congress Cataloging in Publication Data

Shaffer, Floyd, 1930-
  IF I WERE A CLOWN.

  Bibliography: p. 109
  1. Clowns—Religious aspects—Christianity.
2. Christian Life—1960-   . 3. Shaffer, Floyd,
1930-   . I. Title.
BV4509.5.S43   1984   248.4   84-11000
ISBN 0-8066-2082-X (pbk.)

Manufactured in the U.S.A.   APH 10-3198

        3   4   5   6   7   8   9   0   1   2   3   4   5   6   7   8   9

To Marlene . . .
  whose tolerant patience puts a foundation
  under my craziness;

To Sara and Dan . . .
  who still ask what I'm going to do when I
  grow up;

To "the clown" . . .
  Nobody does it better.

Contents

Preface

I can't juggle. I can't ride a unicycle. I can't do clever magic tricks. To compound this reality, I can't even make animals out of balloons. My makeup leaves much to be desired. The pattern for my clown suit is so simple it is found in sewing shops around the country. Even my shoes are unimaginative—just cheap white sneakers. The pom-poms on my headpiece can be purchased at any card and gift shop.

What kind of clown would be so ill-equipped yet presumptuous enough to want to impact the Christian church around the world? Socataco!

Socataco. Even the name started unimpressively—a box of tacos left over from supper and a chance TV show with the oft-repeated phrase "Sock it to me." Fourteen years later, a nun who was a lifelong missionary in Japan shared that an equivalent word in Japanese meant "one who is high on the mountain." See? "Accidents" keep happening and validate the joy of mystery, simplicity, childlikeness, and lots of good things that Jesus says are important.

John Taylor, in his great little book *Enough Is Enough* (Augsburg, 1977), writes:

Human nature as a whole has always been baffled by the peculiarly Christian virtues. At the very beginning St. Paul realized that in face of this inveterate incomprehension we have to expect to be fools for Christ's sake. The word "silly" originally meant blessed, merry, innocent, guileless, holy; but that combination of qualities appeared to ordinary eyes as something fatuous. "Simple" has undergone the same corruption: to be uncomplicated and singleminded is to be weak-minded in the eyes of the world. And the traditional Christian response to all this is to accept the role of clown with gladness. If we are going to keep the light touch in this grim battle and sustain our sense of humour we must try not to be too reasonable. If it flatters us to be called sensible we are lost already, for rationality is the stock-in-trade of the commercial society, for all its basic madness. "It is an irrational act," argued one of the Puritan divines at the time when capitalism was taking wing, "and therefore not fit for a rational creature, to love anyone farther than reason will allow us." Just how reasonable was the cross? So I think we should welcome the outrageous and fantastic into our style of life. It will at least serve to keep us and others laughing (pp. 80-81).

The clown in me stands in awe of such words; I think, "Wow, I wish I'd said that!" Many thoughtful theologians are saying some profound things about clowns. Maybe if I can't *say* things about clowns as well as they do, I could try the next best thing—*be one*! Just maybe the greasepaint, crazy clothes, and silence might in some strange way incarnate the Word—flesh it out, give it substance, and in visual poetry offer the simple message of a God who came and comes in strange ways and who uses many aliases.

So kick off your shoes and join me in a brief excursion of imagination that is being lived out by thousands of bizarre, greasepainted characters who do not know they cannot do the impossible, keep trying, and sometimes make the impossible a reality.

...I'd Laugh
with God

The congregation sat quietly, if not solemnly, attentive. The minister moved smoothly and efficiently through his sermon. Neatly dressed members were statuesque, with the exception of an occasional nodding head—all but one small boy.

He appeared to be about three or four years old, and he happened to be in the pew in front of me. With hands on the back of the pew, he knelt and slowly surveyed the people behind him. A neatly combed head of hair, slightly slicked into place, and large observant eyes made me want to check to see if there were small wings sprouting from his shoulders.

Our eyes met, and I smiled. He smiled back. That generated a larger grin from me, and an even larger one from him. It was a moment no one could have resisted—my mind

immediately drifted from the sermon, and I made a face with distorted grin and crossed eyes.

It happened. The most gentle and soft bit of audible laughter could not be contained as he responded. It was like a partially controlled chuckle, with expelled breath making a sound of delight.

That's when mother entered the story. Hearing the soft noise beside her, and focusing all her attention on him, she gave him a firm swat, and, as tears began to well in his eyes, I could hear her loud stage whisper, "There now, that's better!" I wondered why.

We have no apparent problem envisioning a solemn and rigid God, but just offer the strong possibility of a God who laughs and delights, and barriers quickly arise. Could it be that we seem bent on creating God in our image instead of listening to Scriptures that point to the opposite view? The message is loud and clear: we are created in God's image. Let's pose the possibility that God laughs. Doesn't it seem strange that so many Christians withhold that part of the image from their lives?

You just can't read the opening chapters of Genesis and see a dull and somber Creator. As your mind envisions the twinkling stars, splashing fountains, endless rolling surf, and winds that make the trees dance, a strong sense of delight is evident. When you look at the flowers with their many hues, some with pleasant aromas, others with wild and bizarre shapes, and a few that even eat insects, there has to be a chuckle in response. The animals encourage God's laughter to the surface: the long-necked giraffe, anteaters, a duckbilled platypus, and a most impractical sort of thing— the hippopotamus.

The laughter of God prompts the funniest, lovingest, gentlest action of all when God honors a chunk of soil—a clod from the earth—and bestows to and through it the gift of life. It's interesting that at some later point in history the word *clown* was derived from the word *clod*, meaning "one who is lowliest of the low, called upon to do work that others will not do." Maybe "clods" do have a special place in the wide sweep of creation.

One of the most powerful stories pointing out God's affirmation of laughter and its importance is the Abram story. In the 17th chapter of Genesis, we see God's encounter with Abram. At the age of 99 Abram was given a unique covenant relationship with God; his name was changed to Abraham, and he was told that he and his wife Sarah would have a son. God even named this son-to-be Isaac—a fairly important event, since God didn't name too many people.

There was nothing dignified about Abraham's response. He fell on his face and, with laughter, pointed out the difficulties posed by this situation for a couple whose respective ages were 99 and 90. The freedom of Abraham's response says something about his trust relationship with God. Rarely, if ever, will persons laugh until the tears flow, their stomachs pulse, and their breath comes in gasps as they collapse on the floor unless they are in the presence of someone they trust.

A bit of gentle humor continues in Genesis 18. Sarah was in the tent while the mysterious visitors were reaffirming God's covenant for him. It was there, while eavesdropping, that she discovered she was supposed to have a child, and she laughed about it, somewhat embarrassing Abraham in the presence of his honored guests. Apparently Abraham never bothered to tell her of his encounter with God or the promise of a son. Suppose he had tried. Can you imagine what a wifely response might have been? It would have taken a long time for her to suppress her laughter each time they were together.

Later, in Genesis 21, we read of Sarah's pregnancy and the birth of a son in her old age whom they named Isaac, according to the command of God. With great delight, she proclaimed, "God has brought me laughter, and everyone who hears about this will laugh with me" (Gen. 21:6).

To catch the impact of this, we must recall that a name was understood to be the essence of one's self. It was a word that was "alive" in a powerful way, capturing everything of a person's being. Names were neither given lightly nor without deep meaning. What an amazing glimpse we have of God's character when God chooses the name Isaac. That name literally means "one who laughs" or, if you prefer, "laughter."

Remember how, years later, Isaac had a son whom he named Jacob? Remember Jacob's trickery to obtain the birthright from his twin brother Esau? The name Jacob has the connotation of "the crooked one."

How often we have used the phrase "I am the God of Abraham, Isaac, and Jacob" as if it were spoken with a deep bass voice in an echo chamber. How much more delightful to know God is saying, "I am the God of Abraham, Laughter, and The Crooked One." God's actions in all this must mean that we are allowed something more than a simple smile in church once in a while. One legitimate and holy response we can offer God in faith is our own laughter, for this is a God to whom we can relate, to whom we can extend our total and complete childlike trust. This is a God to whom we can come with our laughter and tears, our joys and our sorrows, our sarcasm and hostility, and even our anger. Abraham could do this with honesty and openness because there was then something that made his connection to God real and believable: he knew he was loved and could be himself.

How tragic it is that many people in God's world continually acclaim other qualities and dimensions of God yet ignore the God who laughs. Might not genuine laughter be more pleasing than the stilted attempts at facial expressions and postures that we try to pass off as reverence?

If I were a clown, I'd want to laugh in those holy moments and know that, despite the sour looks of those in the pews (who appear to have been baptized in vinegar), my nonverbal Alleluia of laughter was praising God in the highest sense, and that it was made more meaningful by the fact that a "clod" could do it.

The ancients were not far afield in their attitudes toward laughter. For many centuries, illness was thought to be of demonic origin. The approach of the "health services" of that day was most unique. They saw a link between that which was deep within a person and that which was necessary to "expel" the demonic. Observation must have shown them that laughter was an "expelling agent." (Notice that when you laugh deeply, you expel breath from your innermost parts.) This forceful expulsion was seen as one way to expel the demonic and make the sick person well again.

It was a custom in many tribal groups that a medicine man or some such healer would dance and prance around a sick person. There was a shaking of wands, the wearing of masks, and weird incantations. We often forget that one of the prime reasons for these antics was an attempt to make the sick person laugh. The logic was simple: "Healthy people laugh; sick people don't." There was the belief that, if a person could be made to laugh, the demon would be expelled and health would return. This rationale could add new insight to movie scenes where the chief is ill and the medicine man is dancing about him. Primitive? Yes. On the right track? Absolutely.

Have you ever noticed that during the neurotic moments of your life all the lines seem to go inward? There is a preoccupation with self. Everything is solemn. Suddenly little problems become very large and consume huge chunks of your brooding moments.

One of the goals in psychotherapy today is to assist neurotics to go outside of the "self," to see possibilities in other things, to expand their interests, to be less afraid—often of fear itself. Genuine laughter can have an important role in reversing the neurotic spiral that pulls us deeper and deeper into self-oblivion. After all, laughter is an outward movement, an expulsion of that which is within, an affirmation of self-acceptance that defies the belief, "I'm too serious about myself."

Is there a message of laughter in the life of Jesus? The clown would at this point roll his eyes and let us know in no uncertain terms that *humor* (derived from the same root word which brings us *human*) was quite evident in the Jesus story.

One case in point occurred when the disciples of the Pharisees and the Herodians approached Jesus in an attempt to humiliate and embarrass him before his followers. They asked him whether it was lawful to pay taxes to Caesar or not. Obviously they knew that whether he answered yes or no, he would be in trouble.

Jesus countered with a request to see the tribute money. They produced a coin and were then asked whose likeness was on the coin. Naturally they responded that it was Caesar's. Jesus then told them to pay to Caesar that which was Caesar's and to God that which was God's.

The humor of the story is often lost because readers do not connect this event to the Old Testament law. It was forbidden to put the likeness of a person on wood, stone, or metal because this would be contriving an idol. Hebrew coins did not bear images of persons, but rather of things of the earth. Since Roman taxes had to be paid with Roman coins, this presented a real problem for the God-fearing Jews—they were forced to use idolatrous coinage. In our story, the would-be humiliators, people well-versed in their religious law, quickly produce a coin. Pause a moment. This coin was an idol to the religious Jews, and here was a purported legal expert in direct physical contact with it. Not only that, it had apparently come from his person, and even the clothing was now believed to be contaminated. The very ones who were attempting to humiliate Jesus were now in contact with, and contaminated by, an idol, and every God-fearing Jew who witnessed the event knew that now there would have to be some rather complicated cleansings done to deal with that fact. We may not like to call Jesus a practical joker, but the picture of these dignified accusers going home to take the complicated baths is not a solemn picture. If I had been there, I know I would have laughed.

Because God does laugh and delight, and because we believe we are created in God's image, we can feel free to let laughter have its place in Christian life. To withhold or suppress laughter in times of joyful praise and worship is not being reverent. It may be Satan's way to confuse us about what a right relationship with God should be. Perhaps a bit more laughter in churches would be a more acceptable sacrifice, one that is sweet to the Almighty!

If I were a clown, *I'd laugh with God.*

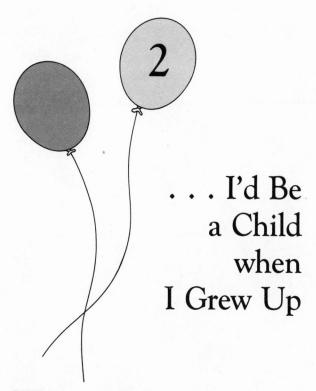

2

. . . I'd Be a Child when I Grew Up

T here was an air of anticipation and excitement in the nursing home. For 10 weeks a group of the residents had been taking a class on clowning. Hesitant at first, aware of their ages and physical conditions, they were encouraged by two of the staff who wanted to share the joy of clowning. They learned about the clown as symbol, worked on makeup, developed skits, gathered costumes, helped each other, and laughed.

Imagine their delight when an invitation came to present a program at an important gerontological conference. Wheelchairs, crutches, and the eight residents slowly boarded a van and were transported to a prestigious university. The program was presented to a delighted audience of

professionals who were aware of many of the dynamics at work within the group.

One of the clowns was a woman approaching 90 years of age. She was without legs, and one arm was paralyzed, but she wore an orange fright wig, a wild hat, and a crazily-put-together costume. Someone asked her about her attire, and she responded with a slightly creaky but bubbling voice, "I can hardly wait 'til next year when I get a new costume." Now that's some kind of hope!

If I were a clown, *I'd be a child when I grew up.*

There's a group exercise that almost always seems to work if I have about 10 persons involved. The group is asked to think of one really good childhood experience. It need not be big; in fact, it may not have been remembered for years. The experience is then shared. Usually we have recollections about wading in water, jumping from high places, making tunnels in leaves, building a "secret" place, parties (real and imaginary), visits with grandma—add your own to these if you wish.

When the stories have been shared, we attach a descriptive quality to each one. For example, to a story about wading in water—feeling a chill on the skin, having the sensation of mud "squished" between the toes, and hearing the sounds all around—we would affix the quality *sensual* (meaning "of the senses"). A party with fresh cookies and cold milk might have the quality of *celebration* attached to it. Burrowing leaf tunnels: *imagination*. Jumping from high places: *risk*. Having someone catch you when you're stuck in a tree: *trust*. Hide and seek: *play*. Sitting in the family car, nestled down between parents: *touch*. Sitting beside a lake to view the sunset: *wonder*. Making a toy from discarded boards: *creativity*.

When all the stories have been labeled with a descriptive quality, we pause to discover that we have been producing partial definitions for childlikeness. Perhaps that is what Jesus had in mind in his emphasis on the affirmation of the child. This must have been what Picasso meant when he said, "It takes a long time to become young."

To become mature is to engage in the process of becoming childlike. Tragically, many persons seem to be traveling in the opposite direction. With their aging comes loss of imagination, limited sensuality, and little celebration; play becomes work, nothing brings wonder, risks are frightening, trust goes sour, celebration is seldom, creativity and imagination stagnate.

Is it any wonder that a clown wants to be a child? One role that clown-type persons assume is that of the "confuser." Taking the values they see around them and reversing them requires a special kind of wisdom, and no example is quite so clear as that of a child. The qualities of a child are seen as supremely worthy, and clowns utilize them to the fullest. Yet in a world where most people strive to be "grown-up," the clown functions precisely at this clash of goals. The clown offers paradox as reality, saying, "To be grown-up is to be a child." The clown's wisdom expresses itself in a deliberate attempt to create confusion in those who do not see the truth of this paradox.

One of many descriptive definitions of a clown is "a vulnerable lover." Most of us prefer to have love occur with no hint of vulnerability on our part because we confuse vulnerability with weakness. Have you ever had the experience of being in a place with people you didn't know? Most of us hold back in opening a conversation that could lead to a relationship, unless it is with someone who communicates strong acceptance. With most people we shy away from eye contact, smiles, touching, and words, perhaps because we feel we may eventually be rejected.

The vulnerable lover knows something special: the important end result is not whether we have been accepted or rejected but rather whether or not we have been risk-taking, caring, outreaching persons.

The clown is keenly aware of this. The clown knows there may be joy and happiness when a person is open and responsive and there may be disappointment when the response is negative. What keeps the clown going is the fact that the goal is neither acceptance nor rejection, but the process of making oneself vulnerable. The clown knows that he or she is making use of values that others may not understand. But it is worth the risk.

In a clown workshop the time always comes for taking "the plunge." Sooner or later, participants put on greasepaint and costumes for the first time and enter the world as clowns. Some interesting transformations begin to happen as the ways of a child are utilized and experienced.

A group of fearful beginner clowns went to a nursing home (a common plunge) and moved by twos into the various rooms. I was privileged to mingle, out of makeup, with the staff and other visitors in the role of observer. One nervous clown had confided to me her previous repulsion toward nursing homes: the smells, sounds, the anticipation of imminent death. The assignment was simple: to see some needs and meet them with the caring, vulnerable ways of the clown who uses exaggeration to mirror reality. She wasn't convinced she could pull it off, but, with a resolute look and a deep breath, down the hall she went.

Her first encounter was with a wizened little man in scruffy clothing whose wheelchair faced a blank wall upon which he gazed intently—perhaps seeing pictures of time past. She offered the man an inflated red balloon with the large word *love* emblazoned on it. Her first attempt seemed to fail. The wall seemed more interesting than the balloon and the colorful, cavorting clown who wanted attention. My heart sank, but only for a moment, for next the clown took the balloon, thrust it inches from his eyes, and pointed animatedly to herself, the balloon, and the aged man in triangular fashion to signify—without words—"I love you." The look on his face indicated comprehension, and he smiled. "You really do love me!" he said, and as she saw that look, she threw her arms around him and planted a very large clown kiss on his cheek. The dry eyes were few and smiles many for those who witnessed this.

Later, when we discussed this, I raised the question of the old man's unkempt condition and the odor surrounding him. Her answer was simple and profound: "I didn't notice—guess love got in the way."

Children, regardless of their age, have a natural sense of being vulnerable lovers. Maybe that's why they have less of a problem with appropriating God's grace—undeserved love—than those who would complicate it with conditions. The very essence of clowns is to offer the confusing, zany connection between child and sage in a journey toward simplicity. Clowns and children alike can understand this short phrase from Bernstein's Mass: "For God is the simplest of all."

Many people have problems with growing up to childlikeness because they confuse it with childishness. Children involved in play are poetry in action. You can see the vitality, the healthy self-love, imagination, fantasy, and celebration bubbling over. Sometimes when they discover they are being watched, there is a shift in the quality of their performance. Is there a parent who has not slipped occasionally when the change was noticed and said, "Stop being so childish!"?

Clowns help the child within us to become "unstuck." One powerful illustration of this occurred at a retreat for clergy and spouses. The premise that directed the program was that few couples had known each other between the ages of four and eight. After some introductory discussion on clowning and its relationship to childlikeness, we played some childhood games. The first one was the old familiar "Tag." One minister was "It," and the game began. Something didn't seem right, so time was called after one minute of playing. When asked who was "It," over half the clergy held up their hands. It seemed that many of them had forgotten how to play the

game and were simply tagging as many others as possible. Here was a small and not too uncomfortable embarrassment that opened an enlightening reflection.

Somewhere, under the illusion that we are "growing up," we make a repressive move away from the child within us and immediately organize our play in such fashion that the spontaneity of play for play's sake is lost. We forget that God created Leviathan, the sea monster, just for the fun of it.

One of the most powerful learning experiences grown-ups can have is to see children at play. The kind of play you find on a rainy afternoon when you are housebound is the best. Perhaps the children don't have a television to watch, and the toys for some reason are not accessible. Let them pull out some pots and pans and, in short order, there is a band emerging as a wooden spoon begins to bang away. An old sheet and a cardtable become a tent. Some can lids are transformed into dishes, and a party begins. A few paper bags and some crayons are soon used to prepare hand puppets, and stories are created and told as an improvised stage appears where there was once just a footstool or a chair back.

 Childlikeness seems to bring out the best in creativity and imagination. Have you ever noticed how many people sit around in committee meetings and bemoan the lack of imagination? Maybe a few children would help!

This became very evident to me at a weekend workshop that I led for clergy and lay leaders. One minister said that he had to bring his young son—about 10 years old—or he wouldn't be able to attend. The "grown-up" in me made me grit my teeth. I imagined all sorts of complications, but an agreement was reached that the boy would participate fully.

We were in the midst of an exercise moving toward self-identity. It was a simple thing that was aimed at "unsticking" the imagination. The first question was this: "If you could be a vegetable, what would you be, and why?"

The grown-ups—all very well educated—had answers like:
"I'd like to be a carrot because it's orange and I like orange."

"I'd like to be a head of lettuce because it's crispy and crunchy."

The boy's turn came. The prevailing attitude was condescending and paternal/maternal. There was a brief moment of silence, and he leaned forward on his chair. Then he said, "I think I'd like to be a peanut, 'cause when you're in a deep, dark place and things are pushin' down around, you've always got a friend."

The silence was deafening. A few eyes looked around the circle and met. I nearly slid off my chair. What wisdom! What insight! What imagination! What "childlikeness"!

Needless to say, when the next questions came (e.g., "What kind of a fruit would you be? What kind of an animal would you be?"), the responses had some substance. The youngster had turned the workshop around and was the pivotal point that opened imagination. Children are awesome, beautiful ministers who have much to share. Maybe that's why clowns want to be children when they grow up.

One moving experience that reminded me of the power of Jesus' statements concerning "becoming like children" occurred in a very large congregation in Minneapolis. I was there for a weekend of workshops and speaking engagements, and I led worship as a nonspeaking clown, interpreting the liturgy through action.

The worship was held in a large meeting room that seated several hundred people. The regular liturgical service was in another place at the same time. The room was packed. Not only were the allotted chairs full, but additional chairs were carried in; folks were even standing around the perimeter. Ushers hastily carried in the tiny chairs used in the preschool department. My working area grew smaller and smaller. Tiny children were sitting with their feet on the platforms in front of me—no aisles!

The liturgy went well. The response was warm. The children were attentive. There I was, leading a liturgy in front of 500 balloons and a makeshift altar—crooked candles and all. It was time for the Communion.

In my usual fashion, I took a towel that had just been used in a handwashing ceremony, gently covered a loaf of uncut bread, and held it lovingly in a rocking motion. I paused to stroke the top, give it a kiss, and put it to my shoulder as if it were a baby. In the front row, an "older" brother—about five years old—whispered loudly to his younger sister, "That's the baby Jesus."

I placed the loaf of bread on a crude wooden cross and let a crown of thorns drop over the top of the bread. The boy whispered once more, "That's Jesus on the cross." With vibrant shaking motions, I broke the bread on the cross, and the boy whispered, "That's Jesus; he's crucified." As I made gestures of offering the broken pieces to the group, indicating "for you," he said, "He's going to give it to the people to eat."

I took the bottle of wine and the cross in hand. As I "poured" the cross into the bottle, the boy said, "That's Jesus' blood." As I displayed the wine dramatically, with gestures symbolizing "for you," the whisper continued: "That's Jesus' blood; he's going to give it to the people."

I could have cried with joy!

After the worship had ended, the balloons had been distributed, the people had joined hands, and I had disappeared to remove my makeup, I reentered the worship area. A fine and loyal man somewhere in his 40s came up to me. His three-piece suit conveyed the authority and power of a business person, a pillar of sorts. He shook my hand warmly and said, "You know what? I understood everything you did. But what was that thing you did with that loaf of bread in Communion?"

I told him briefly, but can't remember what I said. All I could do was remember the words of a five-year-old and wonder a bit about who communes and what intellectual

"answers" are necessary. Then I remembered the words of Martin Luther in the Catechism about who is worthy to receive the sacrament.

"Given and shed for you for the remission of sins."

Maybe a child could lead us.

Do you know what? If I were a clown, *I'd be a child when I grew up.*

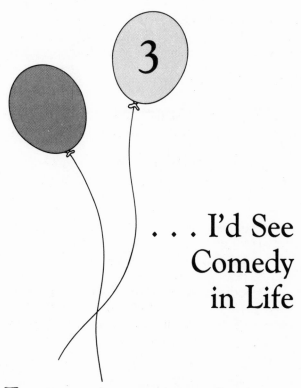

. . . I'd See Comedy in Life

I t happened in the early days of my clowning. A small tent circus came to town, and I stopped by to visit. To my amazement and great delight, I was invited to work in the circus one night. Nothing big—just the "walk-around" (the time before the circus begins when clowns "work" the audience around the arena) and a clown skit or two.

My assignment for the walk-around was the old camera routine. Blocking out a piece of the arena, I looked for someone whose picture I could take. Someone always responds. After a few moves of straightening clothing and flicking hair, I stood back and set off a small flash pot in the camera. After counting down the seconds on a toy clock, an instant photo was removed: a picture of a jackass. Supposedly that is the end of the routine. It didn't feel good, so I posed my "model" again, put a red dot on the cheek, and took another picture. This time I pulled out a "smiley face" with a red dot on it. The participant smiled, hugged, and went joyously back to the hard bleacher seats.

This was comedy. Not just in the put-down, but in the raising up. I was hooked by the concept: If I were a clown, *I'd see comedy in life.*

Pause a moment and think about what you feel comedy is. Most folks equate it with the comic, with laughter the end result.

Comedy is a *process.* There is something very intentional about it. It isn't just joke-telling or laughter-inducement. Comedy can include the tragic and the joyful, laughter and tears, smiles and sarcasm. But above all, comedy *lifts up!*

In comedy there are usually two actions and an actor. The first action can be diagrammed with an arrow pointing down at a 45-degree angle. The second action can be diagrammed as an arrow going up from the base of the first at a 45-degree angle, but going much higher. A small circular line between the two—connecting them—is the representation of the actor.

The first action is the put-down, an action that, on the surface, pokes fun at the recipient. If you stop at that particular point, you have an incomplete comedic situation. There must be the action following that uplifts. The actor almost always is a nonheroic type of character.

Recalling the circus routine just a while ago, the pulling of a picture of a jackass from the camera is the put-down. But when the "smiley face" is produced, the person is raised to a new sense of worth. The actor is the clown, the clod, the fumbling, bumbling, nonheroic character who gives of self to make it happen.

Comedy is something implicit in the essence of life. Historically, clowns were involved in raising people "up" at the expense of self. Perhaps an early application of this principle may help to clarify the concept.

In earliest times, long before events were recorded in writing, people were organized in tribal life. Maybe we could envision a circle as a symbol of the community. Now draw a line down the middle, dividing the circle into two equal parts. On the left side we have those parts of the community that could be labeled "practical." On the right side we have those parts that are called "mystical."

Within the practical dimensions of the community, there was a person called the "headman." Here was the person with a lot of *apparent* power. He generally made decisions about the tribe's activities, its moves, its defense, and its internal problems that needed solving.

Also on the practical side were the "warrior-hunters." Here were the ones who defended the tribe, who sought out the animals in the hunt that would provide food and materials for use in daily life. All very practical considerations.

The other side of the community contained mystical elements. There was the "shaman" who possessed much apparent mystical power. He could look to the stars, interpret the shapes of smoke from the campfire, and determine the way the "forces" were in action. He was in direct company with the headman and the warrior-hunters in terms of pointing the direction in which the tribe should go.

Also on the mystical side was an apparently useless character (not called "clown" at that time in history, but whom we shall call by that name) who was the lowliest of the low. This person was not smart enough to be a shaman, not brave enough to be a warrior, not strong enough to be a hunter, and not powerful enough to be a headman. The clown was the one who did the work others wouldn't do, the one who was the butt of jokes, who was put upon, and who was laughed at.

Of what possible significance could the clown be to balance out the circle that defines the community as being "complete"? Maybe an imaginary story (with documentation from pictures on cave walls) will help:

It is night. The warrior-hunters are gathered about a campfire in the cave. The tribe is low on food and the hunters must go out to slay the great wooley mammoth that has been sighted in the valley just over the third hill. You can tell they are frightened as they sit around the fire. Their physical postures exude anxiety. They know their only weapons are sticks and stones, and they know that some of them may be killed or injured by the great mammoth.

Suddenly, up from the campfire as if a sprite, the clown arises! Going to a corner of the cave where skins of animals from previous hunts are piled, a particular one is chosen. With the skin thrown over his shoulders, with the dried skull over his head, a weaving, dancing movement carries the clown to the campfire. Entering the charmed circle there, he approaches some of the bravest of the brave.

With exaggerated movements and roaring sounds, he pretends to be the animal of the hunt. The hunters look at him and with disgusted grunts wonder what is happening. Eventually one of them swings a stick; another throws a rock, and the clown flinches. After several passes, one of the warriors swings out with his club and the clown backs off, only to follow with yet another mock attack. In a few moments, the warriors rise and chase the crazy character about the cave. When he is cornered, he falls to the ground, bearing the blows of sticks and the battery of stones in a mockery of death. The warriors return to the campfire in gales of laughter, dancing the valiant dance of the hunt.

What has happened? *The clown has taken away their fear by taking it upon himself.* I've experienced this time and time again. Clowns seem able to incarnate the barrier, raise it up, and, in so doing, help people deal with their own situations.

One illustration occurred during a Christmas week when the director of our child-care center invited me to play Santa

Claus. No one nearby had a pillow, and I didn't need one. The older children responded on cue, and it was delightful.

The final room down a corridor contained very young children—ages two years and under. As we drew near to the door, I went down on my knees to look physically smaller, hesitatingly put my hand to my face and my thumb to my mouth, and said softly to the director, "Will they hurt me?" A child came around the corner and handed me his blanket. What a ministry! Here was someone who saw Santa as being more afraid than he, and he stepped in to help.

Still in character, I went slowly and somewhat fearfully in. Toys were handed out. The helpful child stood by, rubbing against my leg, and I lifted him to my knee. A bit of gentle cuddling took place, and we left with a mutual good feeling.

I found out later that this was an abused child who had not responded to touch or affection. After all, the abused child sees touch as painful. Somehow a fearful, hurting Santa raised the child to a position of "power" and, in so doing, enabled the child to minister to someone more hurt and fearful than himself. When we give away our power, a new power is born.

This has happened in hospitals where a child has been afraid of an injection and a clown working with a doctor has exaggerated the pain and suffering to the point of laughter. The child could then receive the injection. Why? Much fear had been removed by the presence of the clown, who was more afraid than the child.

Suddenly the Scriptures speak loudly to us when we recall those words of the prophet Isaiah, "The Lord has laid on him the iniquity of us all" and "by his wounds we are healed." Suddenly the cross begins to make some sense. In this action of being crucified (the put-down), Jesus, in a special, non-heroic way, has raised us up so that we don't have to be afraid of death. He's done it for us and, as in the process of comedy, has raised us up to a place where we can be human, childlike, and ourselves.

The comedic principle can be seen clearly in the Scriptures. In the Old Testament we see many examples of the Israelites confusing ends with means, replacing God's values with their own, and God, working through history, allowing other people (like the Philistines, Amalakites, and Babylonians) to bring them down (the first action of the comedic process).

Working through many nonheroic types (like the judges and prophets—the actors), a reversal action is initiated (the second action of the comedic process), and remnants of God's people are raised to new and higher places with a recommitment to God and the covenant.

In the New Testament we can apply the comedic process to the conversion of Saul. Here he is, persecuting the Christians, when suddenly he is struck blind (first action). Along comes Ananias (the actor), who raises him up to new possibilities (second action), and we have Paul—the greatest of missionaries. There was no magical change, but a real transformation as he was empowered by the Spirit.

Even in the Christmas story we find the comedic principle at work. In fact, it is a real classic, because God becomes *both* action and actor. In John 1 we read, "The Word became flesh and lived for a while among us. We have seen his glory, the glory of the one and only—who came from the Father, full of grace and truth." God comes in human flesh (first action), and now in Jesus Christ, raised up, people can can receive the powerful message of God's love. Jesus (the actor), visually nonheroic, was born in a stable, chose a donkey to ride, and was crucified on a garbage heap outside Jerusalem.

Mary seemed to grasp the naturalness of the comedic principle when, in Luke 1 she sang, "He has brought down rulers from their thrones but has lifted up the humble." Can you catch the sense of comedic rhythm?

The comedic theme continues in the Christmas story as we see the unlikely combination of angels and shepherds. Here we have an angelic choir, messengers from God, singing their hymns of glory to a bunch of simple country folk. Those shepherds must have been an unlikely bunch for the emissaries of the Lord to encounter. The thought of that well-rehearsed angelic music coming to some people who only understood country and western material has its own possibilities for some real humor.

The visit of the Wise Men, bringing their valued gifts, is like a beautiful postscript to the Christmas story. Imagine these men of risk, vision, and intelligence coming with gifts in hand to a humble home. Entering the door (of a typical home), they would be met by a barnyard before they could mount the low platform where the holy family lived. What a beautiful rhythm of action—being humbled but then raised up.

And so it goes for a clown's view of history and life. Is it any wonder that, historically, clowns—often doing bizarre and crazy things—were ultimately concerned with the process of raising people up and doing so at the expenditure of self?

If I were a clown, *I'd see comedy in life!*

. . . I'd Choose My Mask Wisely

For a country boy, going on tour in Australia and doing national television shows is a scary thing. There I was, on tour with one suitcase, a public relations person towing me around, and advertising that was much bigger than I or anyone ever could deliver.

We had just two hours of network studio time to do five one-minute spots for the Roman Catholic community. Being naive, I had decided to do it.

In order to make the best use of time, I decided to write one piece that included going into makeup. It called for me, a weary businessman with briefcase, to step before a large mirror. My hair is combed, my comb drops, and a suitcase with clown material is discovered. The makeup and costume go on—white face, powder, the reds, a rubber nose, black lines, a headpiece, suit, and derby.

At the end of the message, dressed fully as Socataco, I lean forward, look into the mirror, and a voice comes on with the brief message: "Everyone wears masks. Why not choose yours wisely?"

If I were a clown, *I'd choose my mask wisely.*

In a clown class, there comes a time when clown identity is probed. It begins with a few "unsticking" pieces that we mentioned earlier—questions to loosen the thought process and move toward creating a relaxed atmosphere.

The first question is: "If I could be a vegetable, what would I be and why?" The second is: "If I could be a fruit, what would I be and why?" The third is: "If I could be any part of the whole animal kingdom, what would I be and why?" The final question is the homework for the week: "If I could be a clown, what would I be and why?"

Then it's time to pause and look at various clown types in order to stimulate the thought process. We pause and contemplate some of the important aspects of a clown's makeup. For instance, the white colors or the white portion of the face symbolize death. In nearly every race and culture, white markings on the face symbolize death. The Apaches used the color white as part of their facial war paint before entering battle.

From African cultures we learn that when someone dies in a village, often one of the "wise ones" leaves the village, puts white clay on the face, powders it with ashes or dust, and then uses colored mud or the juices from berries to put "life" marks on the face. Then, with crazy clothes that feature feathers, twigs, and bizarre accessories, the "wise one" reenters the village playing, dancing, and cavorting. This is a reminder to all that death has entered the village.

I'm sure this ritual has been an intuitive thing, but what really is happening is a demonstration that reminds everyone that all are human, all will die. Such is the task of the clown: to show that all people are human and mortal.

As I began to realize how universal certain symbols of facial colors were, it dawned on me that here, presented in unusual forms, were the symbols of death/life. In the Christian interpretation, it all makes sense. Clowns—who tend to confuse ideas intentionally—are reminding us that, as humans, we are on a journey from death to life, even though most of the world thinks it's the other way around.

All kinds of recurring statements in the Scriptures emphasize our journey from death to life. We are daily to die to sin and rise to righteousness. Through Baptism we die with Christ, are buried with him, and rise to newness of life.

Suddenly it is very clear! The clown's face, when properly understood, is a message of Easter. It is precisely out of an Easter understanding that the symbolism of the clown's face takes on special meaning. I need to die to myself, even in a symbolic way, to become a clown. Old clothing needs to be replaced. A new face is part of the new creation. The clown becomes a symbol of what St. Paul meant when he said that if anyone is *in Christ* that person is a new creation! And we are asked to "put on Christ." In clowning, as in many things, *form follows function.* Clowns need to pause and consider what the function is to be, and then the form just seems to fall into place.

There are several types of clowns, and some types can even overlap. (Any symbol that deals with freedom and liberation in the way that clowns do cannot be structured around rigid rules.) We'll share some of the main types.

One of the common clown types is the *white face.* Sometimes you'll hear this clown called a "neat" clown. Essentially the face is white, with no more than two features given major attention. The white face is a childlike clown. In many ways, it is the exaggeration of childlike qualities. The white-face

clown is playful, uses simple props, is vulnerable, mischievous, and often takes charge. The key phrase that describes this clown's function is *joy bringer*. Joy bringing does not necessarily always mean laughter, but rather the joy of simple things, including vulnerability, touching, and smiling. The costume is generally colorful and communicates symbols of joy.

The *tramp* clown, often sad-faced, has tattered clothing, torn handkerchief, battered hat, and disreputable shoes. This clown walks with slow movements that convey the weight of the world on the shoulders. The solemn eyes and down-turned mouth arouse a caring instinct in those who come close. The task of the tramp clown is to evoke that caring instinct from people. Most folks want to make a sad person "unsad," and this particular ministry helps people to become caregivers.

The *Auguste* clown is easily identifed by the makeup, which usually includes large sections of white around the eyes and mouth surrounded by flesh tones. There may be a small hat, oversized shoes, and exaggerated parts of the body (hands, stomach, waist, ears, etc.). The Auguste is the clown for whom nothing ever seems to work. Bicycles fall apart. Props collapse. The Auguste gets a foot caught in a bucket or trips over such things as feathers and beams from a flashlight.

The function of the Auguste is that of reminding us we are human. After all, aren't there days when things just don't go right? We laugh at the Auguste and, in so doing, we can laugh at that same quality in ourselves.

Another clown type, not so easily categorized, is the "character." This particular clown takes on the identity of an already known character: a policeman, Raggedy Ann or Andy, or even an animal. Once more, the primary function of the activity determines the makeup and costume.

Very often the choice of clown character has a profound effect on the person inside the makeup. One white-face clown in my first class declared that she would like to assume a more loving identity and chose the name of Lily Love. Usually she would first appear in a sinister cape costume, communicating violence and hate. Then some sort of transformation occurred: through clown technique the cape fell, revealing a happy clown with red hearts emblazoned on a blue sweatshirt. While blowing kisses and giving hugs, she gave away candy kisses.

By her own admission, this clown's clowning changed the way she looked at others about her. Somehow the liberated clown character that helped her to express love toward others had a profound effect on her life. It was like watching a butterfly emerge from the confinement of a cocoon.

Another clown chose the tramp identity. Her story was beautiful. As a pastor's wife in Chicago, she experienced times when ladies' groups from the suburbs would come into the city to "do their yearly thing." Frequently, as the women came to the steps of the church, a wino by the name of Harry would be sprawled in front of the door, reeking of cheap wine. The women had to step over and around him to enter the church. The clown—who chose the name Harry—felt clearly directed to minister to people by letting them become caregivers and remember that "but for the grace of God, that could be me."

The tramp clown, which emerged during the Civil War and was enacted time and time again during various periods of economic depression, was a kind of "sojourner" in biblical thought. These wandering strangers in need of help would find homes that would provide food, a little work, and perhaps a barn roof over their heads for shelter. Even in our affluent society, people's hearts are still moved by the person who comes to them hungry and in rags. They provide a real ministry in enabling us to be caregivers.

A particular Auguste clown who went through an identity shift started out as a white face. Somehow she was not comfortable in the childlike, joy-bringing role this clown required.

She was a professional church worker and was involved through Christian education with hundreds of families. She spoke of the pain and the hurt that they experienced. She counseled with them in areas where they seemed to be slipping around in their lives and falling on their faces. It suddenly struck her, as she looked at them through the eyes of a clown, that people need to be reminded of their humanness—their slips, their falls, their crazy actions—and she decided to be that kind of person. After all, even though the Auguste clown falls a lot, this clown also touches others in ways that help them to stand. In fact, although the Auguste is known by the pratfall, in many clown circles this is known as the clown who can solidly stand.

What an affirmation of grace! We fall on our faces daily in sin, but God, in a gracious burst of love, offers us people and resources that can help us to stand. God doesn't guarantee that we'll never fall again, but when we do, he provides us with the strength to rise again.

For many beginning clowns the makeup becomes simply a mask. In the costume and hidden face, the clown looks out on a world that cannot recognize him or her. In some ways, such a disguise helps persons give permission to themselves to become the people they would like to become.

The thoughtful clown who searches for identity knows there is more. In many situations, the clown characterization is the "permission giver," allowing the person to be who he or she wishes to be. The exaggeration is still there. The bizarre makeup and costume are still there. The overly dramatic actions are there. But behind the facade there seems to be a consent or self-permission that allows us to become like children. Messy faces become welcome. Crazy dress-up clothes are acceptable. Doing things one might not ordinarily do is made possible. Clowning helps us wipe off our slates of life the writing we may not like and for a time helps us be what we'd like to be.

Since clowns are not seen as having either a male or a female gender, there is the intensely positive attribute of no discrimination as a result of one's human sexuality. Remember when St. Paul spoke about not being male or female, but *one* in Christ Jesus? The mask of sexual stereotypes is erased; in fact, the masks of all stereotypes are erased. There are no racial clowns. There are no clowns of a particular denomination. There are no politically specific types of clowns. The careful application of makeup, costume, and function shows our human unity before God. Can that be all bad?

Even the costumes of clowns reflect their humanness. The key word is *diminutive*—from the top down. The white face is beneath a rather nice hat. Clothing is colorful and neat. But by the time you get to the shoes, they have become quite simple.

The same is true of the tramp. The hat may be neat, the coat a bit shabby, the pants covered with patches, and the shoes totally a mess. The lines of direction in costume are "down" or "down to earth." (Remember the word *clown* comes from the word *clod*.)

Even the Auguste, wearing a tiny hat opposite oversized shoes, exemplifies this down-to-earth feature. The attire reflects a flow or theme of smallness and complexity to largeness and simplicity from the top down. The clothing is purposely arranged to communicate that the clown is down to earth.

Have you ever noticed that a person who is kind of "klutzy" is often called a clown? And people you really like are often described as being "down to earth"? Perhaps the similarity in the meaning of clod/clown may really be a compliment. Perhaps that's why clowns are so human, so down to earth.

If I were a clown, *I'd choose my mask wisely!*

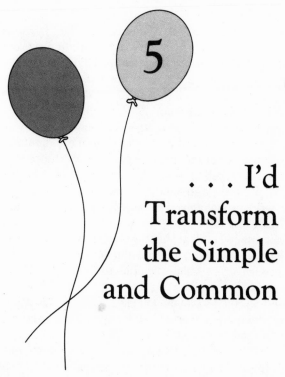

...I'd Transform the Simple and Common

Some of the programs I'm invited to do are more scary than others. Here I was, a major part of a three-day conference for educators and church leaders in education. When it's not your own denomination, and you're the only one on the program who is not a part of the denomination, the anxiety level can swell.

It was the first night. The dinner for over a thousand persons was completed. Songs were sung, welcomes given, introductions made. The denominational president spoke before I was to mount the stage. He was a hard act to follow.

Basically, I had planned to introduce clowning as an educational tool, then enter makeup on stage and do three biblically based "visual parables"—as always, without words.

The audience was warm. They even laughed in the right places. The makeup went on smoothly, and the first routine was very well received. But then I noticed the denominational president sitting near the stage. I went through an internal dilemma: "Should I use him?" "No, you'd better not." "Oh, go ahead!" "You'd better not." "*OK*, I will!!"

It is a rough routine for a large audience. It's done with three matches. Lighting one, I walked into the audience looking for someone. Stumbling, I bumped into the president, apologetically brushing him off, then, as if on impulse (it was!) I took him by the hand and walked toward the stage. The crowd was delighted. In fact, "delighted" was understating their reaction.

He was somewhat ill at ease, but he forced a smile. Taking a match and tearing one side so that it curled upward, I raised one of his arms. The same was done to the other side of the match, and his second arm was raised. The match was split in the middle, and as I pushed his legs apart, it was apparent that the match had become a little symbol of a person, and that, in fact, the match was the president.

I repeated the actions, making a match for myself, clowning playfully in the process. From a burning candle, I lighted my match and the president's match. As we turned them, the flames burned brightly. At the precise "danger" moment, they were placed in a small ashtray. As the tray was raised slowly and reverently, the bright spotlight picked up the wisps of smoke as the matches burned out.

With my finger, I ground the ashes into a small pile and, with simple pointing gestures, indicated that he and I were together in the ashes. Taking his right hand, I signed a large cross from the tip of his middle finger to his wrist and curled his fingers around it as if to grasp it tightly. He did the same to me, and as I displayed my cross to the audience, I moved in a semicircle toward him. His hand came up, the two cross hands came together, and I pulled him toward me. He received the mark of the clown: a little red greasepaint dot on his cheek, and as he hugged me (one of the strongest hugs on record), his eyes brimmed with tears and he whispered in my ear, "I understand."

Later that night we stood on a balcony by ourselves and talked a bit about what had happened. Here I was, a clown, not too bright, and unversed in church politics, with a major church leader—all because of two simple matches!

One of the major tasks of the clown is to understand the meaning of the concept *transform*. Typically, clowns don't "change" things, they "transform" them. In transformation you take the common and simple and raise them to new heights of possibility and meaning.

The roots of this concept are buried in history and even in theology as we see clowns understanding that the most powerful person in the world is one who can give away power. That's the lifting up of others at the expense of self. It's the clown character in prehistory who took the pain of others so they would not feel pain, who became fearful so that others would not be afraid. It's the clown character in the historic circus who, as performers do their death-defying acts, fumbles and bumbles around, doing routines that even members of the audience think they could do just as well. What the crowd doesn't realize is that, as a particular death-defying act is performed, clowns in the area, perhaps trained as paramedics or firefighters, are keeping a watchful eye out in case of emergency. The clown takes the simple and common (the prop, the routine, the self) and elevates it, transforms it to a new dimension.

Just as the simple match became a means for reminding a denominational president that "You are dust, and to dust you shall return" and that out of the ashes the cross is the only hope we can grasp, so the simple clown continually probes the magical concept of transformation.

Most clowns do not perform magic of "power." When they do magic, it usually is done in such a way that the other person is lifted up; the clown remains the "clod." The reason for this is clear. One of the things that makes magic delightful and entertaining is the illusion that, at some point, the magician gives away his or her power. Then the power is taken back and the magician is left as the "all-powerful" one.

Here's where the distinction between *transform* and *change* becomes important: since clowns claim no apparent power—indeed, they seek to give power away—they don't try to change things or people. They *do* work through a process that "transforms" an environment, a moment, or an object.

This fits in well with the way Jesus worked. We don't read about him bragging about his power. In fact, Jesus seems to have been about the business of "empowering" others. A child was held up as having worth. A woman taken in adultery was raised to her feet and forgiven. Dirt and spit were used in a miraculous healing. Jesus even used leftovers in the gift of the Lord's Supper. Can you imagine? Leftovers! Bread and wine from the Passover were set aside for special use with those words, "This is my body. This is my blood."

Jesus' entire ministry was one of transformation. At some point in history, clowns saw this as something that worldly wisdom could never comprehend. They began to act out this concept.

Jesus called a group of people around him—people who were fisherfolk, dreamers, common individuals—and lifted them up in such ways that they went beyond themselves. They witnessed, shared, loved, lived, and died in transforming ways. Through them, the Christian church was born—and continues to make its impact in simple and common ways.

Many of the events in our lives that have had profound effects upon us were simple events. Yet, in a special way, God worked through them to cause powerful transformations.

I remember walking across campus just after my year of internship was served. (I had been sent out a year early because the dean said that I needed to settle down a bit.)

Coming slowly toward me was my former Greek professor, a man in his 80s. He was the one prof we tried to avoid because of his reputation of being "rough," but through him I had learned about grace—the undeserved love of God. He paused and he looked at me with a smile and a little cock of the head. He said, "Shēffer (he never did pronounce my name right), haven't those guys over there (pointing to the seminary facilities) wiped that grin off your face?"

I replied simply, "No," to which he responded, "Don't ever let them do it!"

Here was one of the transforming miracles that shaped my ministry—that somehow it's all right to smile, to laugh, and to be actively at work within the church I love! That professor knew, but it took me many years to understand how people are transformed by the power of God's sense of humor.

Most of my clown routines have a quality of transformation about them. For instance, a sermon may include nothing more than reading a newspaper. The clown looks longingly at each page, searching for the "good news." It isn't found. In desperation, the last section is read: the classified section. "Aha!" the clown exclaims. The want ads are pulled out, and there are the simple words *Help Wanted* printed across the top. A journey through a congregation with searching looks finally moves someone to respond with an upraised hand. As he or she holds the paper, a scissors is used to cut it in such a way that the words *Help Wanted* form the horizontal arm of the cross. The cross is then displayed; my surprised partner receives it and then enables the whole congregation to pass it from person to person.

"If anyone would come after me, he must . . . take up his cross daily and follow me." By transforming something as simple as a newspaper into a cross, a group of typically passive people now share a simple object with great reverence.

To watch a series of newspaper crosses pass among as many as 5000 people is an awesome thing. Somehow the meaning of the text, through a piece of paper, has been driven home: as Christians we are called upon to be cross-bearers.

As we pause to look at such simple events, could it not be that the church is called to be a "transformer" rather than a "changer"? Perhaps we are called upon to create an environment by which the community and world around us are transformed by the grace of God. Just maybe we don't "perform" religion but create an environment to transform people.

If I were a clown, *I'd transform the simple and common.*

... I'd Do Something Intentionally Foolish Each Day

A group of clergy and lay leaders came together in a large downtown church in Detroit. The occasion was a two-day conference to become experientially involved in Acts 2—the beginnings of the church. Preparation included clowns and nonverbal communication, new forms of music, media, and creativity, and a challenge to theological growth.

The entire group was divided into smaller units that, with minimal instruction, were to pretend that the Pentecost event had just happened. They represented the church: a small handful of believers. What would they do?

As one cluster discussed this, someone suggested in fun, "Let's do something religious; let's take up a collection." Conversation circled around the meaning of being "fools for Christ" and the idea of doing something intentionally foolish for Christ's sake. At that point, the idea of a collection sounded reasonable, and the participants good-naturedly dug into their pockets and pooled over $100. Next, two of the attendees were commissioned by the fledgling "church" to go out into the streets and give it away.

The area around the church was one of disintegration— buildings, institutions, even the people carried the scars of loneliness, poverty, and fear. As the two walked, they wondered to whom their gift should go. Should they pass out smaller amounts to many? Should they take it to another nearby church?

Down the sidewalk came a young woman whose clothing and manner identified her occupation. She was a prostitute, a "hooker." They approached her—conversation was not difficult to initiate—and simply gave her the hundred dollars. There was confusion as she asked, "You mean you don't want nothin'? Why not?"

Without being preachy, the two simply said they were part of a Christian group and wanted her to know God loved her. She looked at them, then at the money, and slowly walked away, pausing to look over her shoulder as she turned a corner.

No one ever found out what happened to the woman, but an event like that is not easily forgotten. Somehow we feel that story will be told, and some unlikely people will know about a group who gave her a hundred dollars just because God loves her.

What a foolish thing to do! What a glorious thing to do! What a Christ-like thing to do!

If I were a clown, *I'd do something intentionally foolish each day!*

Sounds crazy, doesn't it? In fact, it seems to violate almost everything we've been taught. But in the Scriptures God affirms what many would call "unusual behavior." To compound our confusion, God seems to be activator and participant in foolish acts. Let's recall just a few of them.

Take a look at Abram's call. There he was, a nice, successful person living in a comfortable community called Ur. It appeared that the chief religion there was worship of the moon god. Yet Abram was directed by God to pack up everything he had and take off for the unknown, where he came to have a unique role to play in God's work of redeeming a fallen world. Abram believed—and took off in faith.

Let's pause a moment and imagine what we might have done if we had been in God's place. How would we have behaved? (Rationally, of course.) I think I'd have personally initiated a "search process" to screen the best minds, proven leaders, and politically astute persons in the world. High-tech assistance would be utilized to speed up the process; computer banks around the world would be tapped. If that were not possible, I'd at least have planned a course of instruction including organizational management, theology, conflict resolution, and a host of other preparatory programs.

But when God chose Abraham he ignored the world's ways of doing things and acted in a manner that seems foolish by our standards.

In so many instances, God seems to contradict all that we deem "logical" and "rational." Take Moses for example. After floating in a pitched wicker basket and being discovered by a princess, he was educated and reared in the lap of luxury among the socially elite in Egypt. Involved in a violent crime and exiled for many years in the wilderness, he returned— speech impediment and all—and led over a million people loaded with personal belongings through the Red Sea and toward a promised land. In spite of Moses' past and his limitations, God used him to accomplish great things.

The book of Judges is filled with unusual choices of leaders. Some of the judges were just plain "irregular" sorts— the kind I would automatically reject on the first round of any draft selection.

There's Jephthah in Judges 11. Of questionable birth status, a victim of strong sibling rivalry, an outcast of his family, he

apparently rose to the top of his profession—banditry. Now this is not the typical, run-of-the-mill person we would expect God to choose. Not only was his occupation a bit unusual, but apparently he was given to making strange vows, like promising God that if victory were given, the first person he saw on return from battle would become a burnt offering. With an eerie, Alfred Hitchcockian twist, Jephthah saw his only child, a daughter, upon arriving in camp. And when he realized the dilemma he was in, he placed the blame on his daughter. Not exactly an ideal image of a religious leader.

Almost everyone knows something about the judge Samson. Once more we would probably question God's choice. Here was an apparently vain, self-centered, spoiled, macho-type person. His life choices were certainly not in harmony with those we would call godly. He was given to violence and consorted with a bad crowd. Does that sound like a wise choice of leader?

One of my favorite judges is Gideon. The story is delightful. In Judges 6, we read that Gideon was threshing wheat in a wine press (?) to hide it from the Midianites. An angel who was sitting under an oak tree came and greeted him with the words, "The Lord is with you." Politely (after all, he was talking with an angel), but with a note of sarcasm, Gideon questioned the angel: if God was with them, why were they having all this trouble with the Midianites? After a miraculous appearance of overcooked meat and unleavened cakes on a rock, coupled with the angel's disappearance, Gideon finally got the point and, with fearful belief, took a step into faith.

Apparently a bit afraid of family and friends, he heeded the Lord's advice and, under the cover of night, tore down an altar of Baal and erected another to the Lord. Gideon sent out his recruiters and gathered an army, but he still had reservations and wanted to check things out with God. To make sure it was really God backing him, Gideon asked for a sign using a sheepskin (vv. 36-40). Here was the test— would the fleece have dew on it one day, even though the ground was dry, and the reverse the next day? God was *very patient.*

Gideon's recruiters had done a great job. In fact, God thought there was an overrecruitment. Gideon had gathered 32,000 men. He must have been proud. And what did God say? "You've oversold—I want my people to know that it is I who am going to win the battle, not your great numbers."

God told Gideon to tell those who didn't want to fight to go on home. We read in Judges 7:3 that 22,000 accepted the invitation! But God thought there were still too many. He told Gideon that the remaining group would be tested. Put yourself into Gideon's mind when the test was determined. It was a simple request to have them get a drink of water. (I would at least have included some multiple choice questions, some fill in the blank, and some true/false!) Anyway, only 300 men passed the test by drinking in a way that apparently indicated their readiness. The other 9700 were sent home.

Sending 300 men against the well-trained Midianite army was definitely peculiar—until you look at God's plan of attack. Gideon's men were told to arm themselves with jars, trumpets, and flaming torches (hidden under the jars). Three groups of 100 each surrounded the Midianite camp. Jars were broken, trumpets blown, torches waved, and shouts raised to thoroughly confuse and defeat the enemy.

Is that a logical or rational way to win a war? It may not seem so to us, but it was God's way. This is just another of the many illustrations of how the apparent foolishness of God is wiser than our human wisdom.

Look at some of the prophets. Their actions often ran counter to the perceived wisdom of the world around them:

* Jeremiah wore an ox yoke around his shoulders and paraded down the street.
* Ezekiel saw wheels in the air and dry bones walking.

✻ Amos, a shepherd and "tender of fig trees," preached a blunt and tactless sermon on poverty and world hunger to the leaders of a foreign country.

✻ Jonah provided us with material for hundreds of Sunday school discussions on whether a giant fish can *really* swallow someone. His reluctance to minister rivals our own.

✻ Hosea married a prostitute (can you hear the gossip?), and when she returned to the bright lights, he went forth to buy all her time. Now *that* is love and forgiveness, but not rationality or logic by human standards.

Jesus' call and sending forth of the Twelve continues to amaze those who search for the rational and logical.

There was nothing rational about the call of St. Francis, Augustine, Luther, Wesley, King, or, for that matter, you and me.

This brings us to an almost embarrassing conclusion. Although I have exaggerated the facts here to get my point across (a technique often used by clowns), based on evidence in Scripture and evidence in the lives of the saints, God does not always act in ways that are rational by human standards!

God is *transrational;* God goes above, beyond, and deeper than our conceited human rationale. Perhaps that is why we often have difficulty with some of Jesus' teachings. To the human point of view, these are *not* rational:

✻ love your enemy;

✻ be a child when you grow up;

✻ give your money away;

✻ take and eat my body, my blood;

✻ I am with you always.

These concepts are *transrational.* But if that is where Christ is, then that is also where we must be.

Perhaps this is where the clown's perception of foolishness can conflict with areas of religion that try to box, package, define, and explain God. A better approach would be to live one's life, knowing that God is in charge and responding to love in foolish ways:

* waging peace with the same fervor that people have waged war;
* loving and serving people where they are, not where you think they ought to be;
* seeing diversity as a treasure to be cherished rather than a cause for separation;
* living with openness to people and ideas instead of being guarded with locked doors of the mind.

Maybe I'd even burn a five-dollar bill to light a candle on a child's cupcake!

If I were a clown, *I'd do something intentionally foolish each day.*

7

. . . I'd Leave My Act Like the Lone Ranger

I t was circus day. A busload of seniors from the church
had planned their monthly outing and received their appropriate discount because of their age. It was like taking a
bus of children on an outing, with everything but the name
tags and mothers-of-the-day in attendance.

As we found our seats, the hucksters demonstrated their
wares of multicolored flashlight rocket guns, balloons that
could be inflated to lengths of up to six feet, and programs
with the appropriate superlative descriptions of the performers and acts.

It was a time for sensory stimulation. *Sights* of strange
equipment, costumed performers who looked like persons
from another world, and bouncing children with shoes flap-
ping because of broken shoestrings abounded. *Smells* of dust

in the air, the pungent aroma of the elephants waiting outside the entrance for the grand parade, and the sweet aroma of caramel corn and cotton candy were all mingled with those of hot dogs, relish, and onion. *Sounds* of people, animals, and a band going through some warm-up songs all spoke of anticipation.

Without fanfare, clowns entered the arena to begin the traditional walk-around—the time before the circus when they "work the crowd" and walk around the inside arena.

There was nothing spectacular about the clowns. In some ways, they looked inept. There were no fancy routines. But they did interact with people and set the stage for the circus to begin.

Then came the parade, with performers in spangled, brightly colored, garish-looking costumes: prancing horses with trainers balancing on one foot as they galloped by, high-wire walkers, trapeze artists, cyclists riding up an inclined wire, jugglers, daring acts announced by the ringmaster. There was even a man shot from a cannon across the arena to a waiting net.

In the midst of it all were the clowns. In comparison to the other performers, they seemed unimportant. Sometimes they even looked as if they were in the way. Then, as suddenly as they had appeared, and without fanfare or applause, the clowns were gone.

If I were a clown, *I'd leave my act like the Lone Ranger.*

At a circus, people generally respond to the performers and the clowns in different ways. They look at the performers doing their death-defying acts and think, "Wow, I could *never* do that!" Then as the clowns come by, fumbling and bumbling, they think, "Hey, even *I* could do that!" Our seniors were no different. Upon comparing performers and clowns, one turned and, pointing to a performer, said to me, "Pastor, why don't you learn to do something like that?"

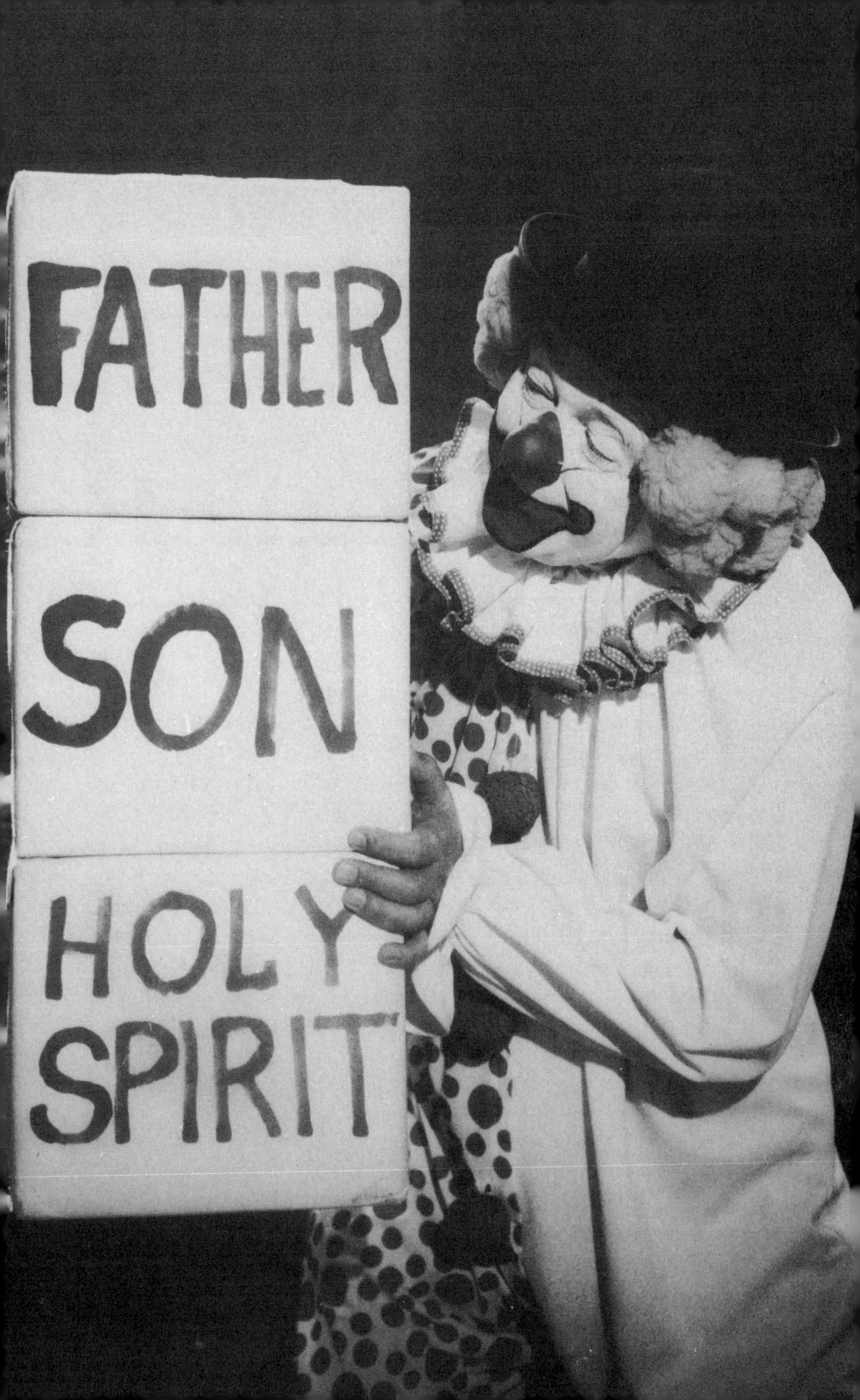
FATHER
SON
HOLY
SPIRIT

In one sense, clowns do "perform" their routines, at least as far as the audience is concerned. In the historic sense, however, clowns are not seen as performers. Performers engage in daring feats with great expertise. Clowns often point out failures or human flaws that, in many cases, are transformed or exalted by them.

Clowns were traditionally hired, not as performers, but as people who used clowning to do a job. Their main task was to create a mood or an environment in which the circus could happen. Without them, there would be no circus. Barnum is often quoted as saying, "Clowns are the pegs upon which you hang circuses." However, they often do other important jobs as well.

In observing this subtle but real distinction, clowns take on new meaning for those who watch them do their seemingly ridiculous routines. For instance, while a dangerous high-wire act is going on, several clowns might stand nearby, just clowning around. One might well be a rigging specialist and the other a paramedic. While clowning, they keep a watchful eye and are ready to act in the event of an emergency, yet all the time creating an environment in which the circus can happen.

Who hasn't laughed at the antics of the rodeo clown? While the "performing" cowboy engages in the task of attempting to ride a bull, the clowns play around until a specific moment. When the rider is finally thrown, it is the responsibility of the clown to offer a distraction and draw the attention of the bull in order that the cowboy can safely get away. As they engage in a buffoonery or imitation of the bull, mock charges, and hiding in the ever-present barrel, they become a kind of "savior." Figuratively bearing the possible pain and injury themselves, they offer new life for the cowboy.

There are many applications of clown roles to the life of the church. For those who lead and participate in public worship, it might be well to consider our task as that of a

clown. We are called on to create an environment in which
worship happens—in which the people of God become *participants* in a joint venture together.

Perhaps a local congregation could see itself as a clown
in the community, creating an environment in which God's
grace can be seen with such clarity that others will think,
"That's for me." Maybe the Christian church on earth could
see itself in the motif of a clown—creating an environment
so rich with love, concern, acceptance, and servanthood that
nations would pause to give thought to that identity.

Creating an environment happens so often in clowning.
There are growing numbers of convalescent centers that
have caught the spark of this concept and are utilizing clowning as one of the humanizing influences that improves the
quality of life.

It all began when several clowns whom I'd trained went
back to the nursing home where they were on staff. An introductory program of visits, crazy hat contests, and balloons
in a party atmosphere set the stage.

A 12-week training program began. It started with the el-
derly sharing stories of their childhood. Activities around the
theme of "Being Childlike—Jesus-style" emerged. Skits were
designed around nursery rhymes, events in the home, and
the holidays of the year.

The skits about the nursing home were most interesting.
As the residents used exaggeration to make fun of painful
things like putting on a back brace, an artificial limb, or using
a bedpan, others joined in gales of laughter. When you take
something that is painful or "bad" and expand it dispropor-
tionately, it becomes funny. Laughing at painful things makes
them a bit more bearable.

Residents learned about makeup and, if physically able,
applied their own. A water-based makeup was used for easy
cleansing purposes. Funny hats, kazoos, rubber noses, and
fuzzy toys were quickly assembled. Watching them parade
down the hall—limping clowns pushing those in wheelchairs

who couldn't walk—listening to them sing to the kazoo accompaniment of "She'll Be Comin' Round the Mountain," hearing the laughter, and seeing the smiles of fellow patients with whom they visited and gave the gift of a smile and laugh, brought flashes of Jesus' words in Matthew 25: "Whatever you did for one of the least of these . . . you did for me."

An idea crossed my mind quickly. For more than 25 years, I'd ministered in nursing homes, bringing Word and sacrament and through them the hope of everlasting life. That's really important. But what about the day-to-day hope of the residents? People who have had some contacts in a nursing home might recall that often someone stops by to see if a person has had a bowel movement. Inwardly and outwardly I laughed as the thought settled in—there ought to be something between the hope of going to the toilet and the hope of everlasting life. *What about next week?*

The environment created by the clowns enabled folks to happily anticipate clown day and the other childlike programs associated with clowning—an anticipation greater than the one felt about tomorrow's TV program or another quiet game of bingo. The creation of this environment reinforced a positive climate and offered a positive quality of life, and it linked believably to the hope of everlasting life.

A clown called Natty Bumpo took a deep breath and began ministering in a residential hospice. With the symbols of life and death written on her face in the colors of her makeup, and with the simplicity of a clown's approach, she went forth—touching, listening, offering a smile and herself wherever it was needed. In a hospice, you can't be content to offer just an object. As in all effective clowning, you offer yourself.

One resident had clowns on the wall—pictures given to her by children and others in her family. When a real live clown came in, it was love at first sight. A relationship of caring and love was born. After a few visits, it was difficult to tell who was ministering to whom. The relationship extended to the members of the whole family. When death came, the clown received a phone call from the family, asking her to stop by the home where all were gathered. She was asked to please come dressed as a clown, since her presence had meant so much to the family during the difficult times.

That's creating an environment!

Detroit has many housing projects for the poor. The physical environment is depressing: broken windows, plumbing and heating that often do not work, many children and youth with nothing to do, people who have never been offered possibilities, people who hunger, and everything else that gets in the way of a productive, liberating life. Curiously, however, there is happiness and laughter there as well.

On Labor Day 1982, several clowns helped plan and participated in a party with a purpose. With one of them playing a trombone and others on kazoos and rhythm instruments, a parade began through the project. People joined in. There were hot dogs and cool drinks, and a general party happened. From this event, interest was generated for a Saturday morning program that would include using the playful arts—clowning, music, storytelling, crafts—all of the "multi-channels" that could be used to communicate to people that they were loved and through which that message could be heard.

Mothers and children in the project came. All kinds of things emerged as the gathering grew: block plans, food programs, community gatherings, and people who cared for each other. One boy with a lot of street savvy came to the art class. He had never been told he couldn't draw, so he simply plunged in. His pictures were nothing less than phenomenal. Within three months, a scholarship in art was awarded to him by a nearby community college. There was no budget for this program, no long period of study. Just a bunch of clowns who didn't know they couldn't do the impossible and somehow made it happen. An environment was created; things happened and continue to happen.

One of the more sensitive and effective of environmental settings is in the area of clown worship, where an entire service (including the Lord's Supper) is celebrated without a spoken word. This service is not intended to be an every-Sunday event, but rather a simple, isolated sensitization depicting what is actually involved in worship.

There was a time—somewhere around the 12th century—when some of the churches in Europe had small doors in the wall of the chancel area. Occasionally, during worship, the door would open and a clown would pop out to interrupt the service. This was known as a "holy interruption." *Inter*ruption is not the same as *dis*ruption. Disruption would have been viewed as sacrilege. Interruption was a consciousness-raising routine. If it were a festive occasion and the congregation was extremely solemn, the clown, using humor, would remind them that such a response was not proper; indeed, such solemnity was inappropriate to the Lord God. The clown would leave almost as quickly as he appeared, and the worship would continue—with a new environment.

My favorite interruption happened shortly after I had been called to my congregation as an associate pastor. To be authentic, no one should know about it, or else it won't be an interruption. Not even the other pastor was to know about this one. During the hymn preceding the sermon, I slipped into the sacristy and quickly got into makeup and costume. Taking a large, red, gift-wrapped box, I slipped around to the back of the church and fell into position behind the ushers, who were beginning to take the offering forward. Unknown to them, I fumbled, trying to get into step. Soft laughter began in the rear of the nave and followed us to the altar. The plates were received, the offertory response was sung, and the ushers returned to their stations. I remained with my gift box.

The other pastor greeted me: "Good morning, Socataco."

I tipped my hat.

"What do you have there? Is it a gift?"

I nodded yes.

"Who is it for?"

I gestured toward the congregation.

"Why don't you give it to them?"

I walked toward the altar, took a bottle of wine and a loaf of bread from the box, placed them on the altar, and disappeared into the sacristy.

The meaning of this skit was clear, and the pastor simply said, "I think Socataco is reminding us that Holy Communion is a special gift." The liturgy continued. Hence, one brief interruption was used to communicate something people often forget: we have a special gift from the Lord in the bread and wine. The disappearance was important. A momentary creation of a special environment was used to remind worshipers of the meaning of that moment.

When an entire worship is celebrated, it is imperative that clowns realize they are not "performing" a program but creating an environment in which the Word is heard through the eyes. They must present the Word with visual clarity so that both head and heart are reached.

Biblical theology reminds us that "Word precedes action." God spoke ... and things happened. The "Word became flesh." So in worship, the Word needs to be placed into action—not just into our heads but also as our lives translate it.

When I conclude a clown worship, I frequently distribute colorful balloons with the word *love* boldly emblazoned on them. The balloons are raised overhead, and everyone joins hands. A swaying motion creates a giant sea of color. A ceiling of love has been raised over the people of God, and they are physically united as one group. While the music plays, the clown liturgist disappears. Music continues, and people often stand waiting for the clown to reappear. Inwardly, they ask themselves, "Now what? Do we let go of hands? Do we leave, or is the clown coming back? Now what?"

The question "Now what?" is an important one. It needs to be asked every time we participate in a benediction. As a result of gathering with fellow believers around Word and sacrament, we must ask ourselves, "Now what?" It is a question that should challenge us to enter a world that God loves. It is a question that should challenge us as we encounter injustice, prejudice, hate, and all that resides in a world that hurts. It is a question that challenges us to be "little Christs" wherever we are: doing our ministry and not waiting for applause.

If I were a clown, *I'd leave my act like the Lone Ranger.* ("Who was that masked man?")

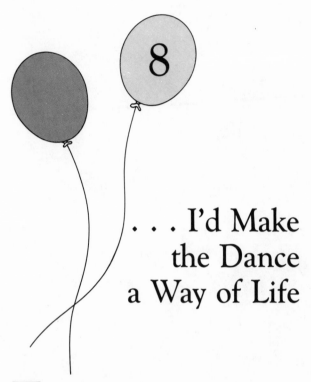

. . . I'd Make the Dance a Way of Life

The 1960s were winding down. Protests against U.S. involvement in Vietnam were rampant. College buildings were burned. Medgar Evers, Martin Luther King, and Bobby Kennedy had died violent deaths. Riots in the cities were common as the flames fanned by frustration and anger flickered against the sky. Lots of name-calling was around us: hawk, dove, nigger, honky, liberal, conservative, red-neck, long-hair, hippy. Grimness abounded.

It doesn't sound like a time for a clown ministry to emerge, does it? Years later I would discover that the clown was an apocalyptic symbol—something that happens in times of hopelessness to remind people that there is hope. For me, this ministry was not extremely well thought-out or planned. It just seemed like a good idea at the time.

Many pictures flash through my mind of those days:

* being accused of not taking a new interdenominational ministry seriously;
* laughing in a meeting that wasn't supposed to be funny;
* walking out of a "heavy" meeting that was going nowhere to visit the local circus;
* grinning at a solemn-faced congregation on Easter morning;
* plowing a backyard in a middle-class community to plant a large garden;
* yawning, and thus causing chaos in my first small-group encounter session.

It makes one wonder whether:
* you can be serious without becoming solemn;
* you can transform groups through creative interruption;
* you can laugh through tears;
* you can be angry without being hateful and hate-filled;
* you can defy custom by providing alternative possibilities;
* you can dramatize celebration by creative access;
* you can question what is happening apart from who is doing it.

There's almost a rhythm at work here, a creative, rhythmic shift, not at all unlike something we call "the dance." As we proceed on our journey through the present into the future (dancing with the world, but inwardly dancing with God), we remember the one called the Lord of the dance.

If I were a clown, *I'd make the dance a way of life.*

There I was, stretched out on the beach of Fort Lauderdale, Florida. The sun was warm. I was lean and tan in those days. The puffiest clouds imaginable were like whipped cream bouncing on the bluest of blue sky. My portable radio was broadcasting the first space walk. This was truly enjoyable ministry, directed by the congregation (so there was no guilt); it was Bethel Bible Day—a day for study and lesson preparation.

I don't remember the book. It wasn't on the required reading list. Maybe it was a magazine article, but it doesn't matter. It redirected my life and ministry. Some writer, name unknown, drew my attention to the fact that the word *clown* is derived from the Anglo-Saxon word *clod*. That's all there was: no bolt from the blue, nothing even as dramatic as the bite of a sand flea working its way on my blanket and up my leg.

It would be some years later that an important lesson would be driven home to me clearly. Most of the really significant events in my life seemed at the time to be small, unimportant moments. The learning process is slow, but the revelation finally came through my thick head: *there are no small, unimportant events.* All are potentially filled with power.

My initial fascination with clowns grew slowly until, at one point, curiosity led me to investigate the possibilities of the word *clown.* I smiled as I recognized that no matter how the opening chapters of Scripture are interpreted, God loved a clod. That lump of earth became something pretty special in God's love and care.

The word *clod* was a term that referred to one of the lowliest members in the community: a lout, an oaf, the one set upon, the one called upon to do the work that others would not do, the lowliest of the low. Wondering if there was a similar term in New Testament Greek, I discovered that among words translated as "servant" there was one special one, *doulos.* Literally meaning "slave," this was the lowest connotation of the word translated as "servant." The *doulos* did the work that others wouldn't do and was seen as the lowliest of the low, until Jesus Christ developed the concept of servanthood.

In the New Testament, whenever Jesus called his followers to be servants or be like servants, the writers used the term *doulos*. This discovery came to me like an explosion. The way the word *clod* (for clown) was used was almost identical to the word *doulos*. In fact, the connection was so strong in my mind, I tried inserting the word *clown* wherever Jesus used *doulos*. Look at what would happen to some familiar verses:

✻ Matthew 23:11—"The greatest among you will be your *clown.*"
✻ Mark 9:35b—"If anyone wants to be first, he must be the very last, and the *clown* of all."
✻ Mark 10:43b—"Whoever wants to become great among you must be your *clown.*"

At this point I paused, wiped my brow (along with the tears of laughter from my eyes), and pondered what it would sound like if, while reading the Scriptures in church, I inserted the word *clown* whenever Jesus used *servant.* I had this weird picture of myself, covered with black tar and feathers, running down the road like a chicken while well-meaning Christians hit me with their Bibles and called me heretical, crazy, or anti-Christian.

It was then that I paused and made the discovery that there was more to the symbol of the clown than someone selling hamburgers or walking in a parade. The journey had begun.

In the early days, I met a circus clown whose gravelly voice was evidence that a hard life had taken its toll. We talked about clown classes and clown schools. After rejecting all those that focused simply upon the mechanics of makeup, costume, props, and skits, he said something that gave me the impetus to begin. As he spoke, his small physical size appeared to enlarge to a stance of someone 10 feet tall. "I've been in this business for 12 years," he said, "and I do not count myself as being a clown, but I am becoming one!" That's all it took. I bought some makeup and took the plunge.

My clown ministry was never meant to be a "program" or a new kind of organization. It just happened. After clowning emerged as the opening for a two-week vacation school, there was involvement in an interdenominational worship fair, some simple interruptions of church meetings, and a neighborhood festival. A Bethel Bible Series teacher-training session of two years was drawing to an end. The group was close, and no one wanted to break the bonds that had begun to grow. One person said simply, "Pastor, what is it with this clown stuff?" I replied that, if she wanted to know, maybe we could have a class. The word went out and 12 people responded.

Now I was faced with what to call it. Doing church bulletin announcements has not been my forte. I like to do them as quickly as possible, so it took about 10 seconds to advertise a class on "Faith and Fantasy." This title later gave me an understanding of the term *dance* when applied to the Christian life.

It was late in the 1950s when I had the pleasure of hearing Dr. Joseph Sittler speak. He said something like, "When you know where you are in your faith, you can launch into the unknown." For someone with a short memory span such as mine, this phrase lay dormant in my brain for an amazing number of years. Finally, the title I had given the class began to take on meaning. The class was about *faith* and ways of living it out as a servant. The *fantasy* was the chosen area—clowning—that would provide the avenue of outreach.

So, for the members of clown ministry, there is an alternation—a connection—between faith, which can risk and experiment into the realm of fantasy, and fantasy, which in turn will feed back into faith. This alternation, this rhythm, was very much the pattern of the life-style of Jesus Christ.

Jesus "alternated" from mountaintop experiences to the more ordinary situations of life. He alternated between corporate prayer with those around and private prayer in the wilderness. He had the occasions to eat in small gatherings with Mary, Martha, and Lazarus and in large gatherings of 5000 around bread and fish. He experienced times among members of the religious community as well as among the publicans and sinners.

A picture began to form in my mind. The alternation between one's faith and the launch into the unknown were not two opposing ideas, but two parts of the same path toward balance. Sports enthusiasts might call it "hanging loose."

The *rhythms* of life and *circles* were two early and important human symbols. (They were also important to the people in the Bible.) A wonderful picture emerges from these symbols. The circle signifies completeness, while rhythms of the world (day and night, rain and shine, cold and warm, summer and winter) all convey a sense of harmony and symmetry.

When you add the symbol of the circle to the alternation concept, and include the idea of rhythm, you have the basic motions of dance.

So Jesus the Christ, living a style of alternation—both God and a human being, in harmony with himself, others, the heavenly Father, and the natural world—was indeed the personification of "the dance."

Jesus promised three things to all people who decide to follow him:

1. They will know joy and happiness.
2. People will think they are crazy.
3. They will probably get into trouble.

Most of us would prefer to stop at the end of point one, never learning what it means to be a "fool for Christ's sake," let alone look into the world for a cross to intentionally carry.

Martin Luther echoed this trilogy of ideas in his theology of the cross: the joy and happiness (point one) follow you as you probe the concept of being a fool for the sake of Christ (point two). Both points one and two apply to you if you decide to take up a cross and follow Jesus (point three).

Perhaps that is why we find it difficult to grasp how the early saints could sing hymns of joy while the flames were licking around their feet, or as the lions raced toward them across the Roman arena.

The journey of the clown is the journey toward the cross. In many classic stories, poems, and songs about clowns, we see four progressing stages in a clown's life: acceptance, rejection, humiliation, and crucifixion. The term *resurrection* is not used because the very makeup of the clown symbolizes the journey from death to life.

A simple story tells about a clown in a village circus who was loved by all. A traveling performer whose daring feats impress all joins the little circus. The clown is rejected by friends and sweetheart in favor of the newcomer. The new performer humiliates the clown publicly, causing the clown to be cast out of the circus (crucifixion). But the clown knows something the rest do not know: there is a circus of life just down the road.

Curiously enough, these themes resound in the Gospels. There are miracles, great followings, and much acceptance. The hard sayings of Jesus follow, and many forsake him. The religious establishment tries to humiliate him with questions about religion and politics, and, when all else fails, it accuses him of associating with the wrong kind of people. Finally Jesus is cast out of the city and crucified.

There is much more to the symbol of the clown than we would like to admit. The rejection and humiliation experienced by a clown are thoroughly consistent with what one might expect in the Christian life.

In one of his country western songs Waylon Jennings says he's glad he's crazy; it keeps him from going insane. Clowns affirm that statement. If what we see in the world is sanity, then perhaps we need to see the world through the eyes of a "foolish" disciple of Christ.

The Christian life, symbolized by "the dance," is a life that moves in harmony with God's will, celebrates God's love, and helps us to smile and rejoice even while we carry a cross.

If I were a clown, *I'd make the dance a way of life.*

... I'd Give Everyone in the World a Big, Red, Love Balloon

Balloons are really something special. I don't mean any old balloon, but the brightly colored round ones. There is always an attraction to holding and possessing for a moment that fragile, colored, rubbery membrane filled with air. Possession of a balloon brings to the surface a sense of delight that cannot be captured in more permanent objects.

Memories of people and balloons fill my mind. Once, after a nonverbal clown worship, people lingered to chat as I began the chore of repacking my props—mostly junky items. As usual, I was perspiring profusely, my clothes were rumpled, my hair was in total disarray, and my face was still greasy from removing the makeup. There were some kind comments, not a few hugs, and many questions.

Two matronly women, wearing pillbox hats and fur jackets, stood patiently outside of the group. Their faces were a bit glum, maybe even stern. Realizing that a clown worship service on Sunday morning may not be for everyone, I was mentally prepared to face their negative comments and criticism.

The others left, and these two women slowly came toward me. The two seconds that it took to begin an anticipated conversation seemed like an hour to me. With a smile, I ventured a "hello." The only comment they made was, "We didn't get a balloon." My defenses dissolved as I asked, "What color would you like?" The answer was immediate and simple, "A red one."

The two balloons were quickly inflated, put on reed sticks, and handed to them. With big smiles, they held their balloons aloft, and, with a perceptible quickening of their step, cheerfully left the chancel, walked down the aisle, and out of the church to who knows where. I could imagine them going out to a brunch of juice, quiche, and fruit salad with the balloons protruding from their purses, just beneath the waiter's curious smile.

If I were a clown, *I'd give everyone in the world a big, red, love balloon.*

My own mother (who, incidently, began clowning at the age of 75) tells the story of the first money she ever spent in her life. It must have been around the year 1907 that she received a whole five cents to spend at the county fair. Looking over the array of possibilities, she bought a red balloon— her very first independent purchase. Somehow the red balloon held more than a simple attraction; perhaps it carried a message.

An experience in Sidney, Australia, stands out as a vivid picture. While doing a number of television shows, our agent arranged for me to do a 20-minute segment on a program that is similar to "60 Minutes." As part of the program, I put the interviewer into makeup, used a spare costume, and offered a clown experience. We were covered by long-distance camera and were wired for conversation even though our encounters with the public were to be nonverbal.

The task was to see if people on the street would accept a love balloon and what, if any, their suspicion level would be.

My first shock, even before we encountered the public, was the change that occurred in the interviewer. This urbane, articulate newsman went through a transformation I could hardly believe. He skipped on the street and made wide-sweeping bows to the staff of a hotel and loitering cab drivers. A large bunch of balloons in hand, we skipped down the street together with the TV cameras concealed around us.

Because I wasn't wearing my glasses, the first two people who were approaching us were a bit indistinct. As we drew closer and I saw them, my only thought was "Uh, oh!" They were young, wearing extremely high-heeled boots, overly short miniskirts, exceedingly tight blouses, and an overabundance of flashy makeup. Their occupation was fairly obvious. Nevertheless, they were attractive in a hard sort of way.

There could be no turning back or denial of their presence. The cameras were rolling and the sound units were on. With a flourish, we bowed and swept the sidewalk before them, and, as we tipped our hats acknowledging their presence, we offered each of them a love balloon. The first one accepted hers with great delight and gave me a gentle cheek-to-cheek acceptance hug. The second one was angry, and her language let us know how much (the words would never make the TV program), whereupon the first chided her and, referring to the word *love* on the balloon, commented in a delightful Australian accent, "Well, at least they're giving it away."

I heard her comment in a different way than she probably intended it, but isn't that what we are about? Giving love away? No strings attached. No price tag. Just giving love away, spreading it where we can. I thought of the many times John writes about love. "Dear children, let us not love in words or tongue but with actions and in truth" (1 John 3:18). Maybe receiving a red love balloon connects with God's grace—love with no strings attached, no charge, just "because."

Even just one clown giving away love balloons seems to multiply the possibilities of spreading love. The greatest number I've used in any one worship service is 5000. They provided the background for a service at the Worlds of Fun amusement park in Kansas City.

There were nearly 5000 youth of the United Methodist Church assembled for a day that included worship at the outdoor amphitheater.

The breeze almost played havoc with our background; I found myself chasing bunches of blowing balloons all bent on leaving the stage. Worship came near its conclusion. Assistants distributed the balloons to everyone. Hands were joined, and the sea of color was breathtaking across the hillside arena. As the youth left the service to catch a few more rides in the park, they began to give their balloons away to other visitors. All around the park people were carrying the balloons—with smiles on their faces. Some questions were asked by the curious. Answers were supplied by the youth. It worked better than a tract; it opened relationships.

The balloon wasn't much in terms of cost, but it provided an opening for friendship. It was a gift and it allowed a relationship to happen. I'm not sure if anything great or statistical resulted. I do know that youth were enabled to give a little love away and some nice things happened.

Why is something as simple as a balloon an effective tool of ministry? Perhaps the answer lies in what happens when a balloon is inflated. Very simply, you blow it up. You impart your breath into it and it becomes what it was intended to be.

There is an interesting Hebrew word that is found in the opening chapters of Genesis. In fact, it's in the second verse of Genesis 1: "Now the earth was formless and empty, darkness was over the surface of the deep, and the *Spirit* of God was hovering over the waters." Not being a Hebrew scholar, I must rely on others who have explained to me a fascinating detail. The Hebrew word *ruach* can mean either "breath" or "spirit." The translation can easily go in either direction without changing the meaning. We see the beauty of this in Gen. 2:7: "And the Lord God formed man from the dust of the ground and *breathed* into his nostrils the *breath* of life, and man became a living being."

Breath/spirit have to do with life force. Their presence is life. Their absence is death.

The clown simply incarnates this symbol. When a deep breath of God's air that circles the earth is taken, transported through the respiratory system, and then put into the balloon, the balloon becomes "alive" in that it is fulfilling the function for which it was made. The clown "breathes life" into the balloon. Perhaps the balloon has the word *love* upon it, and now the balloon becomes an active symbol of love.

When love is rejected, or when another's love is destroyed through thoughtless acts, the effect can destroy the environment in which it was allowed to flourish. This became vividly clear to me at a service for about 300 youth in the earlier days of my clown ministry. The service had progressed well. The congregation was perceptive, responsive, and completely participating in all that was happening. The silent message of a growing and developing love silently permeated the church.

In the midst of a beautiful moment, two boys near the front broke each other's balloons and then broke the balloons of several others around them. The sounds of the exploding balloons were deafening! What had been an experience filled with positive worship energy suddenly changed. You could feel it.

Because this was not *inter*ruption, but rather *dis*ruption, something had to be done. Clowns deal with problems in a different way than most people. Leaving my place, I approached them. Holding the sticks with the tattered remains on the ends, I mimed sadness. Moistening a finger, I touched it to my cheek to indicate a tear. With sadness rather than judgment, I acted on impulse. The service had included placing a red dot on the cheek of each worshiper, using a stick of clown makeup. I gently reached out to each of the boys and, with a thumb, wiped the red dot from their cheeks. The service concluded, and I disappeared to the sacristy with a feeling of failure.

As soon as the makeup was off and the costume folded, a soft knock came on the closed sacristy door. The two boys stood there with downcast eyes. They had not been prompted by an advisor or pastor to find me. Very simply, they said, "We know now what it meant. Could we have our red dots back?" I gave them their dots along with another balloon. With a "high five" handshake and a big thanks, they disappeared on the double to join other members of their group.

Somehow, spoken words might not have done the job. Instead, a love balloon and a red dot opened a door. As the boys left, I uttered, "Thank you, Lord," which left me feeling a lot better.

If I were smart and scientific, I think I could do a research project to discover the connection between an upraised hand holding a balloon and the smile muscles of the face. It's difficult to walk in public, balloon overhead, without a delightful, smiling countenance.

Wouldn't it be great to gather the leaders of the world together, give them each a love balloon (in the appropriate language), and have them walk through the United Nations Building?

Wouldn't it be fun to have our Congress open each session with a balloon launch?

Wouldn't it be fantastic to have all the world's professional theologians leave their studies at the same time, with a bunch of balloons in their hands, and wouldn't it be great if they gave them away to the people they saw on campus?

Wouldn't it be a joy to attend a children's Christmas pageant and see there, sticking from the hay in the manger, a red love balloon?

Wouldn't it be joyful, when we enter the gates of heaven, to have Jesus there, handing us a balloon with a hug?

I believe that something very much like that will happen.

If I were a clown, *I'd give everyone in the world a big, red, love balloon.*

And if you were a clown?

Clown Makeup
for Beginners

The uniqueness of clowns calls for individuality in makeup. Persons who wish to begin should know that there generally are shifts in design and form as a clown character develops.

Many styles of makeup application exist. As skill develops, some of the beginning techniques are put aside as improved methods are tried and adopted.

What I offer here is but one method. If your interest continues, consult experienced clowns for their suggestions and ideas. You may wish to take a makeup class if one is available in your community, or you may simply want the joy of self-discovery.

A minimum number of supplies will get you started as a white-face clown. Even though you wish to have another clown identity, the makeup of the white face will offer essentials of application, design, and experience.

For starters, you will need:

1. A mirror
2. Tissue or soft paper towels
3. Vegetable oil or baby oil
4. Oil-based clown white
5. Black makeup pencil
6. Carmine red lining stick or Carmine red makeup with a 1/4-inch brush

7. Child's white cotton stocking filled with baby powder
8. Soft brush (shaving brush or soft powder brush)

These items are available in theatrical supply shops and most costume stores. Many novelty stores also carry basic makeup supplies. Use the Yellow Pages! If you do not live near a city, order some from sources mentioned in this book.

When you put on your first face, don't expect a professional look. I usually have folks put on a white face and draw or paint the desired features as an initial experience. The second time people are invited to be more specific in details. The first time experience of makeup application tends to build confidence and offers a "feel" for using heavy or bright makeup.

It's time for your first "plunge" into the greasepaint. Ready?

Look into your mirror. Move your facial muscles in exaggerated ways. Reacquaint yourself with your face. Which parts move best? What unique features might be highlighted?

Using the makeup pencil, draw some of the features lightly, then move your face to see what happens to them. If you want to change, just wipe the makeup off and try again. When you have a tentative idea, draw it on paper so you won't forget.

Make sure your face is clean—use soap and water. (Men, a smooth shave really helps!) After your face is clean and you're ready to begin here are some preliminary steps:

1. If you have dry skin, use a small amount of moisturizing cream—no oil!

2. If your clown white is a little hard from cool weather or a bit too stiff to the touch, put a finger scoop in the palm of your hand and work it gently to soften it to body temperature. Many clowns use the white directly from container to face.

3. Apply a thin coat of white over the entire face and areas where skin might show around your costume. The

amount depends on your skin texture. None of us are alike. Dry skin tends to absorb the lanolin in the makeup, so you'll have to use more. A basic rule is to use as little as possible yet still achieve the right degree of whiteness. You can always add a bit more, but it's hard to remove if you apply it too heavily.

4. To give a smooth look, use your fingertips and pat your face completely. This will fill in the thin spots, move some of the thicker spots, and remove the streaks. I find that at this point, another patting with fingers dipped lightly in cold water (just a few drops) helps; this is optional. For a really smooth finish use a small piece of soft foam rubber with a flat and fairly "tight" side. Wet it, squeeze moderately, and "dab pat." You'll soon see the difference.

5. Using the powder bag, pat your face gently, remembering not to tense muscles in your face. Pat the hard-to-reach spots and check to see if any shiny spots show. Powder may also be applied with a fuzzy (lambs wool is great) puff. Tap the puff gently, letting powder sift on face. Then pat gently and thoroughly. Allow the powder to set the makeup for a few moments, then brush off excess powder with a soft brush.

6. Using the red lining stick or makeup with brush, paint your mouth and any other areas you wish to color. A white-face clown generally does not put color beyond the upper edge of the upper lip. Many leave the upper lip white. This provides more mobility of the muscles around the mouth and dramatizes the movement.

7. Powder the colors, then brush off excess powder.

8. Using the black makeup pencil (or, if you wish, a narrow brush with black greasepaint), outline the major features that you have colored or draw any black features you wish.

9. Splash your face with cold water. You may use a sponge (just splash it all over but don't rub) or spray it with a spray bottle. Use a tissue to lightly blot the drops of water. The cool water removes flecks of powder that the brush missed, helps set the makeup, and brightens the colors.

That's an oversimplified description of the procedure, but then it does take some practice. Here are a few added ideas:

1. A white-face clown will emphasize only two features of the face (e.g., mouth and nose, mouth and eyebrows, etc.). More than two will become a "grotesque white face." It's also better to start with smaller features; you can always enlarge them.

2. Keep red colors away from the eyes. Not only is it potentially harmful to the eye, but red around the eye area has a tendency to make a clown appear angry.

3. Some clowns apply powder between each color application. Others apply the white "cut out" areas with cotton swabs or small sponges, paint in colors, and powder all at once. The advantage of the latter is the ability to correct mistakes with the swabs while makeup is "wet." Once makeup is powdered, it is difficult to correct.

4. There are clowns who cut their larger features out of contact paper, stick them to the face, and then apply the white makeup. After the powdering procedure, they can be peeled off and a neat clean design is left for colors. Still others (like myself) draw the large features and apply the white around them. The colors to the unwhitened skin will be brighter than those applied over the white. Do what works for you!

5. The tramp clown is a fairly easy face to learn once you've mastered the application of makeup. Simply use

white for the mouth, flesh-tone makeup on the upper face, and black for the "whisker area." After powdering, draw a few brow lines, crow's feet at the outer edges of the eyes, eyebrows that slant outward, and blush a little red on the cheeks and nose. The same general procedures of makeup apply—smoothing, powdering, and a cold splash at the end.

6. The Auguste makeup requires more work. Generally speaking, you have white areas around the eyes and mouth in an almost unlimited number of possibilities. After the white is applied, a variety of flesh tones may be used around them. Many darker skinned people will not need this. From then on, wax creative. A few brushes will help accent the lining, a big red rubber nose may be added, or a pair of oversized ears.

This section is not intended to be a complete nor thorough explanation of makeup. It's just intended to be a beginning for those who might wish to try it sometime. Remember, form follows function, so some thoughtfulness about your clown character will enable the forms of makeup to make a statement if you wish.

About Clown Skits and Routines

Generally a clown skit or routine is a short, quickly delivered message or interaction. Not every clown should expect to hold the attention of a group of people for extended periods of time. Since our task is to create an environment, and the "mission" should be clear, it can take many forms.

Something as simple as a paper bag could get you started. While it becomes an entertaining routine, it has some strong therapeutic results when applied properly.

Simply take a bag, approximately lunch-bag size, insert your index and middle finger over the inside of the bag's opening edge. Put your thumb firmly against the bag and against the middle finger. Then firmly snap your fingers. There will be a soft pop, and the bag will jump slightly, creating the illusion that an object has been tossed into the bag.

The delivery varies with the imagination. In nursing homes, it only takes a moment to have lonely, physically impaired persons toss an imaginary ball to the clown. Think what is happening. Not only is imagination at work, but there is delight, a smile, and arms moving that often refuse to cooperate with physical therapists.

When you teach some of them how to do it, they have received a gift to share with friends and relatives. A simple gift? Yes! But aren't they often the best kind?

Another item that clowns can use to good advantage is a child's bubble-blowing outfit. (It's even fun to shop for one!) A large wand (generally about eight inches in diameter) can waft a large bubble over the heads of people. With a few blowing gestures, a clown can soon have a group of individuals chuckling with delight as they try to keep it in the air.

Going beyond the first activity, the clown remembers the rule of giving power away. Perhaps by blowing too hard, no bubbles come forth from a small wand. With exaggerated frustration, sadness, and disappointment, the clown invites persons to blow as helpers. When the bubbles appear, the delight of the clown and others is enough to gently affirm the helper.

Simple? Most certainly so! Remember, the clown is there to create an environment and help others to be "lifted up" by giving away power. Too often we look for the grandiose events, the spectacular, the earthshaking moments, and we forget the possibilities of foolishness and simplicity as we minister in a variety of ways.

The Scriptures lend themselves quite well to nonverbal clown messages. There is so much concrete communication—visual imagery—that can be translated into action.

Here's an example of a clown sermon, done without spoken words. It's the first one I ever did, and it has been used in a wide variety of groups and situations. Based on 1 Cor. 12:12-27, it is called "The Body of Christ." Since clown routines are a bit difficult to describe adequately (they change each time with improvisations), you'll have to use a little imagination.

The clown selects a helper from the congregation. Together they walk to the chancel and stand facing each other. Using the old Sunday school children's finger play and rhyme:

* Here is the church,
* Here is the steeple,
* Open the door

✳ And see all the people,

the helper is led through the routine. (Remember how it goes? Fingers entwined together, index fingers raised for the steeple, then the opening of the hands to expose the upright fingers.)

The congregation is invited to join in, and the clown, with hand shading the eyes, looks to make sure all are involved. Then, miming smugness and pride (by strutting with thumbs in lapel area of costume), the clown indicates with pointing motions that a church is going to be built. (Simply shape the church in the air with hands, make the steeple, and put an imaginary cross on top.)

Stepping to the side, a pile of six boards is produced and dropped in the center of the chancel. A toolbox is discovered, but, with comic searching, only one hammer and one nail can be found. The single nail is shown with frustration and sadness. (How can you build a church with only one nail?) Nevertheless, the smugness returns with an "I can do it" attitude.

The boards are displayed one at a time. On each board, the name of a Christian denomination can be seen. Applause is requested as the clown mimes with hands clapping. Each denomination is applauded, saving the host denomination until the next to last board. The final board has the words *etc. etc. etc.* on it (to be inclusive). If you are in your own congregation, or any single-denominational group, this will need some modification. (Perhaps the different committees of your church?)

Laying one board on the floor of the chancel, the clown hammers, adjusts, and makes it "just so." The second board is put upright on one end, with the helper holding it firmly with one hand. A third board on the other end will be balanced with board four across the top. Acting like a builder—checking for straight lines, tapping with the hammer—the clown takes the two remaining boards and leans them on

top of the structure to form a steeple. The helper holds one
with the remaining hand. (A paper cutout of a bell could be
attached with tape.)

With a little concern, the clown debates where to pound
the one nail. The decision is made, and it is pounded in an
absurd place—the end of the board on the floor. With a great
flourish, the clown gestures to the "work" and takes a bow
to applause. Turning to the helper, a similar gesture is made.
Taking the helper's hand to share in a bow, they both move
away from their building, and the structure collapses.

With a look of disappointment, the clown views the rubble
and produces a sign that reads "Is There a Carpenter in the
House?" It is shown to the congregation as the clown looks
them over. Pretending to see one, a second sign is shown
that reads "From Nazareth." With gentleness, the two signs
are leaned where all can continue to see them.

This simple message communicates that Christians dare
not forget the carpenter of Nazareth—Jesus Christ—who
unites us in one holy Christian church as the master builder.

Another simple yet powerful message is based on 1 John
3:18: "Dear children, let us not love with words or tongue
but with actions and in truth."

The only prop needed is a balloon with the word *love*
clearly visible. Each clown has a special way of blowing a
balloon. Some can pretend to have great difficulty and enlist
the aid of the congregation to help blow it up, taking a moment to make sure everyone is involved. When the balloon
is ready, it should be displayed clearly so that all can see the
word *love.*

A helper is selected from the group. As the clown and
helper face each other, the clown points first upward, then
to the balloon, and next to the helper. (Remember how as a
child you thought God was "up"?) The beginning of the message is simple: "God loves you."

As the balloon is held by the clown, some "pointing questions" (no pun intended) are asked without words. "Do you

love God?" (pointing to helper, balloon, and then up). With some folks—especially clergy types—I'll wipe my brow with a "whew!" as they nod yes.

A second question (by pointing), asks, "Do you love these people?" A pat on the shoulder for affirmation is given.

The next question is, "Do you love me?" The clown can playfully respond to the nodding yes.

The final question is delivered thoughtfully and slowly. "Do you love yourself?" I've experienced all kinds of answers here. Some heads nod yes, a few nod no, and some lift hands and wrinkle the brow with a "not sure" reply.

Regardless of the answer, the love balloon is given to the helper with a hug. Leading the balloon-carrying helper to the front row, a worshiper is invited to stand. The balloon is passed with a hug; the next person stands, and love is symbolically shared throughout the group. In large groups, I'll bring out some more balloons and the sharing will take place throughout the congregation.

Just a balloon? Yes, but the means to share the peace and love of God in a gentle way that can subtly involve the most "antitouching" church folk in a most comfortable way.

Skits that deal with Christian concepts can also be visualized. Think of the possibilities in the "separation-reconciliation" motif if we pause and, through the eyes of the clown, look at the absurdity of human choices between sin and God's grace. Sin drives wedges between one person and another, individuals and God, persons and the world around them, and even the self. When we compare the results of sin and God's gifts, the choice becomes evident. Once more, the clown can use exaggeration to demonstrate this.

The simple props are: a piece of chalk, an eraser, and a crow call (or kazoo). Identifying the chalk (perhaps by writing the word *chalk* with an arrow pointing to it) the clown walks down the aisle. Starting at the rear of the group, an invisible chalk line is drawn as the clown carefully backs down the aisle toward the front of the group.

After the horizontal line of separation is drawn, it is continued in a vertical line as high as the clown can reach. Then, wedging the fingers in the imaginary vertical line, the clown separates it as if it is a heavy curtain. Wiping the brow from the effort, and stepping through the imaginary curtain, the clown indicates with motions the separation of the group into two parts. The group is now seen as divided—if only in the imagination.

Next the clown communicates to one-half of the group the fact that a solo will be played using the crow call or kazoo. After a very brief bit of raucous noise, applause is invited. Usually there is a very small amount. Then, jumping over the "chasm" that divides the group, the same action is repeated. There is always more applause (groups tend to compete).

Turning to group one the clown delivers a "raspberry" with tongue extended toward them in mock disgust. Back over the chasm the clown goes to repeat the routine, this time beginning with group two. Generally the applause and cheers of group one outdo the other group. The "raspberry" sound is repeated toward group two.

This is repeated three times on each side of the chasm, and often the competition becomes quite heated.

After the third time, the clown produces an eraser and shows it while walking down the aisle to the rear. With wiping motions, the entire imaginary line is erased, and the clown steps back through the hole in the invisible curtain.

The curtain is dramatically and slowly drawn together and erased. The imaginary fragments are brushed together on the floor, slowly raised with both hands cupped together, and gently placed on the altar.

After a wide and slow-moving gesture that sweeps across the group, the clown holds one finger up (indicating "you are all one") followed by a large signing of a cross (in Christ Jesus).

The same absurd noise of the instrument is made, but this time the entire group responds—often rather dramatically.

(I was once carried into the audience by an enthusiastic group of teens.) A simple thrusting of both arms upward concludes the routine in an action meant to convey "Thank you, Lord."

Some clown ministry routines, such as those described, are directed toward communicating a specific scriptural truth or Christian teaching. Whether or not a person chooses to enter makeup and create a pantomimed parabolic message is not as important as what happens when Christians learn to "visualize" events in their minds.

Sunday school teachers can use the visual imagery of the clown to add the quality of imagination to lessons. Clergy can apply the techniques of visualization in sermon preparation and class presentations. Bible students can catch new glimpses of meaning from treasured readings.

God has given us the gifts of imagination and creativity. All our senses are involved in hearing and communicating the gospel. We need not be afraid to use them, but rather enjoy them as a treasure from a loving God.

Resources

Books

Berger, Peter. *A Rumor of Angels.* New York: Doubleday, 1969.

Bergson, Henri. *Laughter.* Bound together with *Essay on Comedy* by George Meredith. Magnolia, Mass.: Peter Smith, 1956.

Cohen, Daniel. *Creativity: What Is It?* New York: M. Evans, 1977.

Cousins, Norman. *Anatomy of an Illness As Perceived by the Patient.* New York: Bantam, 1981.

Cox, Harvey. *Feast of Fools: A Theological Essay on Festivity and Fantasy.* Cambridge: Harvard, 1969.

Disher, Maurice W. *Clowns and Pantomimes.* Salem, N.Y.: Ayer, 1968.

Doran, John. *History of Court Fools.* New York: Haskell, 1969.

Erasmus, Desiderius. *The Praise of Folly.* New York: Penguin, 1971.

Hyers, Conrad. *The Comic Vision and the Christian Faith: A Celebration of Life and Laughter.* New York: The Pilgrim Press, 1981.

Kaiser, Walter. *Praisers of Folly.* Cambridge: Harvard, 1963. Out of print.

Keen, Sam. *Apology for Wonder.* New York: Harper & Row, 1969.

Kipnis, Claude. *The Mime Book.* New York: Harper & Row, 1976.

Maslow, Abraham H. *The Farther Reaches of Human Nature.* New York: Penguin, 1976.

Miller, Henry. *Smile at the Foot of the Ladder.* New York: New Directions, 1975.

Moody, Raymond. *Laugh after Laugh: The Healing Power of Humor.* Staunton, Va.: Headwaters Press, 1978.

Nouwen, Henri. *Clowning in Rome: Reflections on Solitude, Celibacy, Prayer, and Contemplation.* New York: Doubleday, 1979.

Radin, Paul. *The Trickster: A Study in American Indian Mythology.* New York: Schocken, 1972.

Raudsepp, Eugene. *More Creative Growth Games.* New York: Putnam, 1980.

Saward, John. *Perfect Fools.* New York: Oxford, 1980.

Shaffer, Floyd, and Sewall, Penne. *Clown Ministry.* Loveland, Colo.: Group, 1984.

Torrance, E. Paul. *Guiding Creative Talent.* Melbourne, Fla.: Krieger, 1976.

Towsen, John. *Clowns.* New York: Dutton, 1978. Out of print.

Wisse, Ruth R. *The Schlemiel As Modern Hero.* Chicago: University of Chicago, 1980.

Films

(The following four films are available from the Audiovisual Departments of Augsburg Publishing House in Minneapolis, Columbus, and Los Angeles, and from Mass Media Ministries, 2116 N. Charles St., Baltimore MD 21218.)

A CLOWN IS BORN (15 minutes) Features Floyd Shaffer as Socataco

MARK OF THE CLOWN (15 minutes) Features Floyd Shaffer as Socataco
THAT'S LIFE (8 minutes) Features Floyd Shaffer as Socataco
PARABLE (22 minutes)

(The following three films are available from Mass Media Ministries.)

THE BOX (16 minutes)
MINNIE REMEMBERS (5 minutes)
MR. PASCAL (7 minutes)

(The following film is available from Audience Planners, Merchandise Mart, Suite 1358, Chicago IL 60654.)

THE CLOWN OF FREEDOM (30 minutes)

Filmstrips

(The following filmstrips with tapes are available from Contemporary Drama Service, Box 7710-G2, Colorado Springs CO 80933. Cokesbury also distributes these.)

INTRODUCTION TO CLOWN MINISTRY (Floyd Shaffer)
BE A CLOWN (basic clown types and costumes)
CLOWNING FOR KIDS (involving children)
PUT ON A HAPPY FACE (clown makeup)

Slides

MAKEUP TRAINING SLIDES with tapes are available from Clowns of America, 2715 East Fayette St., Baltimore MD 21224.